AN ILLUSTRATED HISTORY OF

IRISH
SONGS & MUSIC

Megan Ó Súilleabháin

Acknowledgments:

Redferns Music Picture Library: p. 4-5, 29, 38, 55, 60, 73 and 114 (Redferns); p. 24 (David Redfern); p. 25 (Brigette Engl); p. 118-119 (Nicky J. Simms); p. 102-103 (Tony Russell); p. 20 (Patrick Ford Fleadh); p. 57, 104 and 117 (Mick Hutson); p. 96 (Harry Herd); p. 101 (Ebet Roberts); p. 108 (Ian Dickson); p. 106-107 (Suzi Gibbons); p. 115 (Erica Echenberg).

The Irish Picture Library: p. 12, 19, 22, 28, 43, 44-45, 53, 61, 63, 67, 70-71, 76-77, 90 and 99.

Christopher Hill Photographic: p. p7, 10-11, 17, 23, 30, 32, 39, 46, 50-51, 65, 66, 97, 109, 111, 112-113, 121 and 123,

Published in 2003 by Caxton Editions
20 Bloomsbury Street
London WC1B 3JH
a member of the Caxton Publishing Group

Designed and produced for Caxton Editions
by Open Door Limited
Langham, Rutland
Editing: Mary Morton and Colin Shearing

Title: An Illustrated History of Irish Songs & Music
ISBN: 1 84067 470 9

AN ILLUSTRATED HISTORY OF
IRISH
SONGS & MUSIC

Megan Ó Súilleabháin

CAXTON EDITIONS

Contents

Contents

Introduction

"I find among these people commendable diligence only on musical instruments, on which they are incomparably more skilled than any nation I have seen. Their style is ... quick and lively, nevertheless the sound is smooth and pleasant."

Giraldus Cambrensis 1146-1230

The above quote is one of the oldest accounts of musical performance in Ireland.

During the past decade, the media has focused a great deal of attention on Irish traditional music but, despite this exposure, its history still remains in obscurity for the general public. The purpose of this book is to shed light on the social history of the immense body of work of Irish music and its musicians. We shall be tracing this history from its early beginnings in the Neolithic and Bronze Ages, through the myths and legends of the Celtic peoples. Even though modern Celtic music has no historical basis whatsoever in the music of the ancient Celts, there is nevertheless a thread of pipe and harp music common to all Celtic peoples, both ancient and modern. The early Gaelic-speaking peoples adopted Christianity and grafted it onto an archaic pagan world and with Christianity came literacy. Before this, the tradition was strictly oral and it was only with the coming of Christianity that the stories and songs became written down through the monastic tradition.

During medieval times and later, Irish music was prohibited and many musicians were imprisoned. During the plantation of Ulster, the Scots settlers brought with them jigs and ballads and their espousal of English culture led to the dispersal of ballad sheets containing popular English and Scottish songs. During Cromwell's brutal resettlement, the traditional distinctions between the native Irish and the old English were removed and musicians began to fill the ranks of the unwanted masses that were exported to the West Indies and the New World by Cromwell's bureaucrats. During the Williamite wars a huge repertoire of Protestant marching tunes evolved, which are still played in modern-day Ulster.

Equally, during the time of the Great Famine, called by some the Great Hunger, many musicians emigrated to America, Canada and Australia where the tradition continued. There it has thrived and been through many changes and innovations.

Its rich and diverse history shows that Irish music has always embraced change and has been enriched by it through the centuries.

7 *Above: Traditional Irish music being enjoyed in and Irish pub in Dublin.*

Story: The Piper and the Puca

A long time ago in Dunmore, County Galway, there lived a piper who was only half a fool. He loved his music but he was unable to play more than one tune himself and that fine tune was the "Black Rogue". However, he managed to make a goodly living by playing for the gentry.

One night he was returning from a dance having had enough drink to make him merry but not to knock him to the ground. When he came to the little bridge near his mother's house, the feeling came upon him to play the "Black Rogue" again when suddenly a Puca came up behind him and threw him on his back. Luckily, the piper managed to get a good hold on the long horns of the Puca and said to him, "Plague upon you, you nasty beast and let me home, I have a ten-penny piece in my pocket and I'm on my way to buy my mother snuff."

"Never mind your mother," said the Puca, "but hold on tight for if you fall you'll not only break your pipe but you'll break your neck." Then the Puca said to him: "So will you play for me? So will you play for me? Shan Van Vocht!".

"I don't know it," said the piper who only knew the one tune.
"Never you mind whether you do or don't, start playing and I'll make you know," ordered the Puca.

The piper strapped on his bag and began to play music that even made himself wonder. "Upon my word, you're a fine music teacher," exclaimed the piper, "but tell me where you're for bringing me?"

"There's a great feast in the house of the Behnsidhe on top of Crough Patric tonight," says the Puca "and I'm for bringing you there to play music for the Sidhe. Take my word for it, you'll be paid for your trouble."

"Well, by my word, you'll save me the pilgrimage that Father William put upon me to climb Crough Patric because I stole a white goose from him last Martinmas."

The Puca flew him across the hills and bogs until he brought him to the top of the Crough. The Puca stamped three times with his foot and a great oaken door opened and they passed together into the finest room that the piper had ever seen. There was a golden table in the middle of the room and hundreds of old women sitting around it. The oldest one arose and said: "A hundred thousand welcomes to you Puca of November, and who is this you brought to us?"

"The bestest piper in Ireland," says the Puca.

The old woman then struck a blow with her staff on the ground and a door opened in the side of the wall and the astonished piper saw coming towards him the white goose that he had stolen from Father William. "By my conscience then," says the piper, "me, my mother and myself ate every taste of that goose except for one wing that I gave to Red Mary and I'm sure it was she that told the priest that I'd stolen his goose."

The goose cleaned the dishes from the table and carried them away and the Puca said to the piper, "Come now, play some music for these fine ladies."

The piper played and the women began to dance and they danced until they could dance no more. Then the Puca said to the women, "Now you must pay the piper." And every old woman drew out a gold piece from her purse and gave it to him.

"By the tooth of Patric," said the piper "I'm as rich as a lord".

"Now come with me," said the Puca, "and I'll take you home."

The Puca stamped three times on the floor and the great door opened. Just as the piper was going to ride off on the Puca the white goose that he had stolen came up to him and gave him a new set of pipes. The Puca flew the piper back to the little bridge near the house of his mother in Dunmore and said to him: "You have two things now that you never had before, you have sense and you have music."

The piper knocked upon his mother's door, saying: "Let me in, mother, I'm as rich as a lord and I'm the best piper in Ireland."

"You're drunk," said the mother.

"Indeed I'm not," said the piper, "I haven't drunk a drop all night." And so the mother let him in. He gave her three gold pieces and said: "Listen now to the music I'm going to play you."

He put wind in his new pipes but, instead of music, the sound that came out of them was as if all the geese and ganders in Ireland were screeching together. It was so awful that even the neighbours were woken and were calling after him to stop, until he put on his old pipes and played the sweetest fairy music for them. Then he told them of his adventure that same night with the Puca and the Behnsidhe. The next morning, when his mother went to look at the gold pieces all she found were the leaves of a plant. The piper went to Father William and told him the story but the priest would not believe a word of it until he played his new pipes and the screeching of the geese and ganders began again.

"Get away from me, you thief," says the priest.

And so, to prove to the priest that his story was true, he buckled on his old pipes and played a beautiful fairy melody and from that day onwards until the day he died there was never a piper in the whole of County Galway as good a piper as he was.

9

11

Above: Newgrange – the most important
Megalithic site in Ireland.

Irish Music in Ancient Myths and Legends

The Early Irish

Ireland has been occupied since Megalithic times but the Irish that are known to the modern world, and often erroneously called the Celts, arrived in a series of invasions, starting as early as 2000 BC.

The aboriginal people of Ireland were called the Fomors and no one really knows where they came from or how long they had been there. Legend has it that these were giants. The word *fomor* suggests that they came from overseas. The first invasion of Ireland was by a group of people called the Parthelon who seemed to be of Greek origin. All of them died out in a plague. These were followed by the Nemed and the Firbolgs, who consisted of the tribes of Domnu, Gaillion and the Bolgs, which means "men of the bag" because they were reputed to carry a bag of native soil with them. These tribes comprised the first Celtic invasion.

Around 300 BC a group of people called the Tuatha De Danann or the Laigan arrived and became known in legends as the fairy people because of their superior knowledge and intelligence. They fought with the Firbolgs and divided up the country of what is now Ireland. The last group of invaders was called the Milesians, ancestors of the Gaels, reputed to have travelled up from Spain. Their bard was called Amergin and his poetic challenge has reverberated down through time ever since. All of these groups form the basis for many of the supernatural and mythological aspects of Irish history.

Above: An elaborately carved stone at Newgrange. 12

Duan Amhairghine

Am gáeth tar na bhfarraige
Am tuile os chinn maighe
Am dord na daíthbhe
Am damh seacht mbeann
Am drúchtín rotuí ó ngréin
Am an fráich torc
Am seabhac a néad i n-aill
Am ard filidheachta
Am álaine bhláithibh
Am an t-eo fis
Cía an crann agus an theine ag tuitim faire
Cía an dhíamhairina cloch neamh shnaidhite
Am an ríáin gach uile choirceoige
Am an theine far gach uile chnoic
Am an scíath far gach uile chinn
Am an sleagh catha
Am nómá tonnag sírthintaghaív Am úagh gach
uile dhóich dhíamainí
Cía fios aige conara na gréine agus linn na éisce
Cía tionól na rinn aige, ceangladh na farraige,
cor i n-eagar na harda, na haibhne, na túatha.

Amergin's Challenge

I am a wind across the sea
I am a flood across the plain
I am the roar of the tides
I am a stag of seven tines
I am a dewdrop let fall by the sun
I am the ferociousness of boars
I am a hawk, my nest on a cliff
I am a master of poetry
I am the most beautiful among flowers
I am the salmon of wisdom
Who alone is both the tree and
the lightning striking it
Who is the dark secret of the dolmen
not yet hewn
I am the queen of every hive
I am the beacon on every hill
I am the shield over every head
I am the spear of battle
I am the ninth wave of eternal return
I am the tomb of every vain hope
Who knows the path of the sun, the phases
of the moon
Who unites the divided, enchants the sea,
regulates the mountains, the rivers, the
tribes.

Irish society consisted of a number of small kingdoms called Tuathas. By the late 11th century these kingdoms were replaced by a handful of powerful provincial kings vying for control over the length of Ireland. The mythological split of Ireland into five parts, with the High King based in Tara in the centre, conveniently allowed the mythologists to place the various tribal groups into a caste system similar to India. In the north were the warriors, in the south the artists, in the west the legislators and intellectuals and in the east the farmers. This caste system would probably have been brought from India along with the Indo-European language, and although inoperative today still underlies the zeitgeist of the Irish.

The Bards

Under ancient Irish laws, social status was denoted according to the number of colours on garments; the peasantry and lower orders were allowed one. The principal nobility were allowed to wear up to five colours, while the bards were allowed six and only royalty wore seven. As high as the profession of arms was held among the Irish, it is therefore clear that the bards were more highly respected.

Seven centuries before the Christian era, the renowned statesman and philosopher Ollamh Fodhla made a law that physicians, poets, genealogists and harp players must be descended from only the most illustrious families in the whole country. In this aristocracy of intellect, there were four principal bardic orders, the highest being that of the poets. They were called Ollamhain, Re Dan or Filidhe. The Filidhe were also heralds who accompanied their chiefs in war and marched at the heads of their armies, surrounded by the Oirfidigh or instrumental musicians. The Ollamhain also had the duty of composing birthday odes as well as lamentations for the dead. The second order of bards were called Breitheamhain. These were a legislative body whose duty was to dispense justice and frame the laws. The third order, called Seanachiadhe, were the historians and genealogists. They recorded important events and preserved the genealogies of their patrons. The fourth order were called the Oirfidigh who were performers on the various kinds of instruments.

The term bard is rarely mentioned in Irish manuscripts and when it is used by Anglo-Irish or English writers it is used solely with regard to the poets. The heads of each of the bardic orders were called Ollamhs. They, as well as their wives, enjoyed special privileges. They were given land and salaries by their patrons. The Ollamhs of music, or those raised to the highest order of musicians, were obliged by the rules of their order to be accomplished in the performance of three particular classes of music: the Suantraighe which was soothing or sleep-inducing music, the Goltraighe which were laments and the Geantraighe which was joyful music. It is recorded that Daghda, the great chief and druid of the Tuatha De Danann, on the recovery of his harper Uaithne and his harp that had been carried off by the Fomorians on their retreat from battle, achieved these three musical feats.

Over the course of time, the bards, since they were of the high caste, became involved in the misfortunes of their chieftains and people, firstly becoming personal attendants of impoverished chiefs and finally becoming wandering minstrels, partaking of the hospitality of the reduced aristocracy of this ancient race.

15   *Above and left: Druid Bards depicted on ancient coins the ones on the left show a lyre player.*

Ancient Instruments

The earliest surviving instrument found in what is now Ireland is a Stone-Age whistle found on a beach south of Dublin, of a similar design to an ocarina. Many of the standing stones found throughout Ireland, when struck, produce bell-like tones and it is highly likely that Stone-Age man used stones to make music.

Bronze-Age remains of various horns made from bronze, cast at the earliest around 1500 BC, have also been discovered. These are small, heavy and relatively plain in appearance, but as the casting expertise improved over time more elaborate and larger designs were made and have come to light. The horns were cast using the "lost wax" method, using clay moulds.

These horns required an enormous amount of skilled labour and wealth to produce and it is likely that they were highly valued at the time. The bronze horns were blown gently and produced rich harmonics and overtones, making their sound mellow, haunting and deeply evocative. Irish horns are unusual in that part of their configuration is a large, open mouthpiece which allows the player to produce a variety of sounds and tones, using circular breathing, which can give a powerful rhythmic feel. Battle horns have also been found which are made from long cow horns. These were played by blowing loudly to create impact with volume.

The most likely use of the Bronze-Age horns was in sacred ceremonies. There is every reason to suppose that musicians during this time in Ireland came together to swap tunes and play sessions, very much as they do today. This idea is further reinforced by the recent discovery that most of the surviving original horns have a common tuning and relative pitch to each other. There has been a movement to revive their usage in modern-day music by reconstructing the horns to the original specifications and using what is known of modern rhythms and existing present-day indigenous instruments and music from other cultures, for example the Australian didgeridoo.

In Irish mythology the supernatural tale of Tain Bo Froech, or the Driving of the Cattle of Froech, relates how music made by the horn players of Ailil, the King of Connaught, was so wonderful that 30 of his men died of rapture.

Above: An Irish standing stone.

The Harp of Cnoc-Í-Chosgair

O harp of Cnoc Í Chosgair

that bringest sleep to eyes long wakeful,

thou of the sweetest and delicate moan,

pleasant, refreshing, grave.

O choice instrument of the smooth, gentle curve,

thou that criest under red fingers,

musician that hath enchanted us,

red harp, high-souled, perfect in melody.

Thou that lures the bird from the flock,

That coolest the heart,

brown, sweet-talking speckled one.

Fervent, wondrous, passionate.

Godfraigh Fion Ó Dálaigh (1320–1387)

History of the Harp

Harps are the oldest known string instrument. The bow harp can be traced back to 3000 BC in Egypt and Sumeria. The bow harp is made from a single piece of wood, usually cedar, and strung with gut like a bow and arrow, with three to seven strings of different lengths to create different tunings. Bow harps are still used today in parts of Asia and Africa.

Examples of the Angle harp have been found in Sumeria dating from as early as 3100 BC when it was called *balang* and was the chief instrument in religious ceremonies. In Egypt the harp was the instrument of the cow goddess Hathor and was called the *tobuni*. There is also mention of stringed instruments called Kinnor and Nebel in the Bible. The association between King David and a harp did not begin until medieval Europe, however.

The Greeks had harps but Plato felt that they had no place in an ideal society as they did not contribute to the strength of the mind, body or spirit. There is also evidence that the Romans possessed harps.

The earliest Irish harps can be dated to about 540 BC. They were known as *clarsach* or *cruith* and were carved from a single piece of wood. A translated text suggests that they were made of willow. Around 500 AD stories abound that the harp was being played in the halls of Tara.

It was in the Middle Ages that harps strung with strings made of brass and steel (see the Brian Boru harp) were used. Harps were played with fingernails and gave out a long, sustained bell-like tone. They were usually played over on the left shoulder, not the right as in modern practice.

The harpers of Ireland had a distinctive place in society and were always treated like dignitaries. The golden age of the harp in Ireland was the 12th to the 14th centuries, when bards used harps to accompany songs, poems and epic stories. During the reign of Elizabeth I, as we shall see, harps were burned wherever they were found.

19

Above: The Brian Boru harp.

The Brian Boru Harp

The Brian Boru harp is the national symbol of Ireland and is also used by Guinness as their logo. It was originally strung with 30 brass strings and had a range of four octaves. It would have been played in the traditional way with long fingernails. The original harp dates back to the 15th century and is on permanent display in the Library of Trinity College, Dublin. It is the oldest surviving Irish harp in the world and was named after the Irish High King Brian Boru who was a renowned harper and bard.

Above: The Brian Boru harp.

20

Brian Boru (Brian Boroimhe) was born in Munster in 940 AD and was one of Ireland's greatest leaders. He battled against the Viking raiders of the time. He hated them with a vengeance because as a child he had witnessed the death of his mother and much of his tribe, the Dal Cais, at their hands. Although his older brother Mahon was King of Munster and had attempted to make peace with the Norsemen, Brian Boru would have none of this. He waged guerrilla warfare against the Vikings and, after many successful attacks, his brother renounced his truce with the Vikings and many Irish men joined Brian's cause. They managed to drive most of the Norse from southern Ireland. Ten years later they returned and captured and killed King Mahon. Brian succeeded him to the throne of Munster and set about, once again, purging the country of Vikings.

He killed their king Ivar in single combat, then set about rebuilding many of the churches and other monuments that had been destroyed by the Vikings. In 998 AD he met with Malachy the Second, King of Meath, and they agreed to divide Ireland between them. Because of Brian Boru's popularity, even in Northern Ireland, Malachy eventually allowed Boru to take over his lands peacefully and Boru was granted the title Ard Ri, meaning High King, in 1002, thus uniting Ireland for the first and last time under one monarch.

In 1013, Maelmordha, King of Leinster and others of Boru's rivals held a revolt and allied themselves with the Vikings. On Good Friday 1014 at Clontarf the revolt culminated in a battle in which almost 4,000 Irishmen were killed. However, the Norsemen suffered even greater losses and were forced to retreat. Before all the invaders fled, a small group came upon Brian's tent and murdered him. Ireland then fell into chaos with their High King gone.

The clan O'Brien are said to be the descendants through Boru's four wives and 30 concubines.

"Brian Boru's March", which commemorates the Battle of Clontarf, has been played and recorded by many Irish traditional musicians, including the Chieftains and Clannad.

21

Above: Brian Boru.

History of Bagpipes

The bagpipe has been and is still played all over the world. It was referred to in biblical times. The Egyptians called it *zouhara*, the Greeks *askaulos* and the Romans the *tibia utricularis*. In Wales it is called *pyban* which is a similar word to *pipai*, the generic name for all types of bagpipes in Ireland and Scotland.

The pipes were among the favourite musical instruments at the great triennial fairs at Tara which continued from pre-Christian days to 560 AD. The earliest depiction of bagpipes in Ireland is shown on the High Cross at Clonmacnoise, dated 910 AD. Mention is also made in Irish writings, later on in the 10th century, of pipers attending a king's funeral.

The bagpipe belonged to the Celtic peoples, and can be traced all the way from ancient Scythia via the Black Sea and the Mediterranean to the shores of Ireland.

It was used as both an instrument of war and of peace. The war pipes called the Piobmor of the Gael were carried into battle. No single musical instrument ever devised by man united in itself so wide a range of utility as the bagpipes. It pealed forth merry melodies in the halls of the chieftains, at the birth of heirs, at marriages, and at other festive gatherings. It has, from remote times, given laments and a melancholy wailing at funerals and no other instrument gives expression to grief the way the pipes do.

The uillean pipe (pronounced illyan) has been developed from the early 1700s to the present time and is probably the most elaborate bagpipe of them all. The word *uillean* is the Irish for elbow and describes the way it is played, using the elbow to blow the bellows bag. It differs from the warpipe in that the warpipe is mouth-blown and the uillean pipe is bellows-blown. It is also called the union pipe.

Above: The High Cross at Clonmacnoise, dated 910 AD.

22

The most important feature of the uillean pipe is its melody pipe or "chanter" which plays more than two complete chromatic octaves. Most other bagpipes can play little more than one. The chanter itself is actually a primitive form of the oboe. The pipes have three drones, the same as Scots Highland pipes, but the most unusual feature of the instrument is the set of three, four or five-note stopped harmony pipes. The keys are operated by the wrist whilst the piper makes fingerings on the chanter, thus providing several simple chords for accompaniment. These harmony pipes are called "regulators". The most commonly heard pipes are tuned in the key of D. The drones are also all tuned to D and the chanter plays two chromatic octaves, starting with a D. Sets of pipes before the late 1800s were played in the keys of, B and B-flat. These pipes were not so loud and were nearly always played solo as it was difficult to tune other common Irish instruments to them.

To play the uillean pipes the piper must be seated with one leg lowered; the chanter bottom is placed onto this leg in order to seal the opening shut so that the piper can either play continuously or stop the chanter to play staccato notes.

23

Above: The uillean pipes.

History of the Flute

Flutes have been a feature of rural Ireland since the time when it became possible to bore holes in wood or pick up a hollow stem. A flute would be the cheapest instrument for rural peasants to make and play and was widespread in its use. Because of this association, its significance in Irish music was overlooked until the classical flute was invented and imported into Ireland from Europe in the 19th century. Indeed, the flute player's status was low until modern times when James Galway elevated its status by playing traditional Irish music but in a classical way with the Boehm metal flute.

However, in general, the wooden Irish flute is the preferred instrument as it has a full, rich and mellow sound quality. It is made with fewer and larger holes than a classical flute as Irish music does not need all the chromatic notes, nor does it need the shrills.

Above: James Galway playing the Boehm metal flute.

History of the Fiddle

The fiddle evolved from several instruments, including the violin. The earliest documented reference to the violin was in 1523 in Italy. It developed from the Rebec which dates back to the 13th century in the Middle East and had three strings tuned in fifths. The Renaissance fiddle had five strings and produced a great sonority of sound because of the way it was designed. It had a soundpost and flat sound box with a separate neck and fingerboard and therefore was easier to play.

The actual construction of the fiddle is dominated by laws of acoustics and physics and nothing much can be changed in this without disturbing its fine balance as a work of art.

Although it is uncertain when the fiddle first arrived in Ireland, it has been played there for over 300 years.

25

Above: A fiddle player.

The music of Ireland, particularly fiddle playing, can be defined in the same way that the dialects of Ireland are defined. Although the Irish language is not as widely spoken nowadays, where it is spoken, the accent and dialect differ and this is reflected in the local style of fiddle playing. For example, the Ulster area has a flatter tone and staccato style of playing, in accordance with the tone and rhythm of voice in that region. As we move further south geographically, the style becomes lighter and more fluid. A summary follows of the various regional musical styles:

Ulster – North Donegal/North and Western Tyrone
The style is fast-paced and aggressive with a sense of urgency and power owing to the influence of the Scottish settlers.

Ulster – East Derry/South Tyrone/Antrim
A slower type of style, but slightly more elaborate, again featuring an aggressive element because of the Scottish influence.

Ulster – South Donegal/Fermanagh/North Leitrim
The southern part of Ulster has a slightly bouncier feel although it is still powerful and assertive in style.

Connaught – Sligo
The music is characteristically fast and its mood is light with the rhythms being bouncy, enabling much toe-tapping and dancing. This area most influenced the American style as many of the people of Sligo emigrated to New York.

Connaught – East Galway
The style is moody and played in flat keys. It is highly ornate but gives an impression of sadness.

Munster – Clare
The slow pace of Galway is reflected here but it is less eerie and more melodic in its charm.

Munster – Kerry/Limerick/Cork
Here we once again find a fast pace of music, with a greater range of musical emotion, full of light melodies perfect for dancing to. The distinguishing mark of the area is the polka style, along with the slide.

Leinster
This is the area where the aristocracy could be mainly found and therefore no particular fiddle style is associated with this province. The harp dominated this province, however.

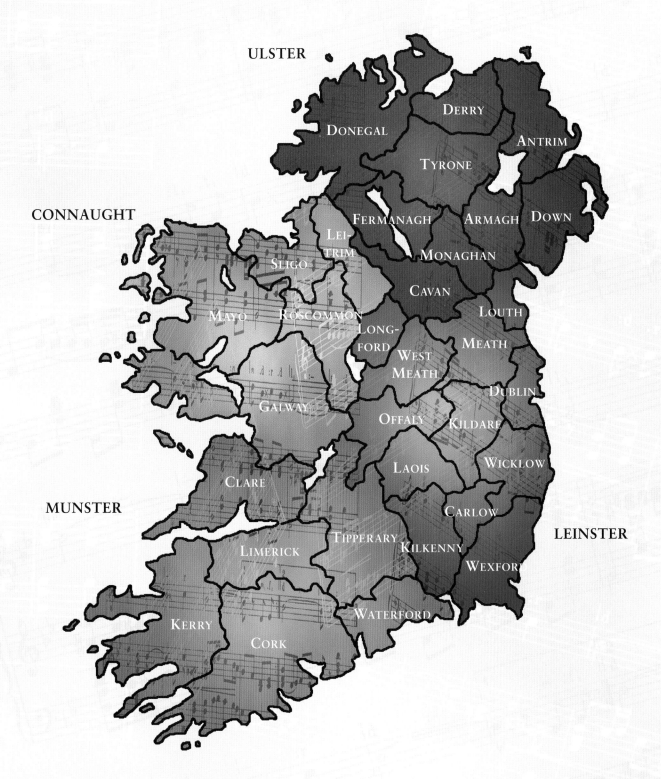

27

Above: Map of Ireland showing the four provinces.

History of the Bodhran

"Ireland uses and delights in two instruments only, the cithara (harp) and the tympanum."

Gerald of Wales in 1185

Although the bodhran as we know it today is a modern instrument, the above quotation shows that drumming has always been a part of Irish traditional music. The bodhran itself seems to have evolved from the tambourine which is heard on Irish music recordings dating back to the 1920s. The Mummers of south-west Ireland also used handmade drums for theatrical effect and the war drum has always been carried into battle in order to make a lot of noise to intimidate the enemy and stir up emotions within the troops.

Other theories as to the bodhran's origins suggest that it came up from Africa through Spain, was brought by the Milesian invasion or originated in central Asia and was brought to Ireland by Celtic tribes – or even that it originated in rural Ireland, evolving from the improvisations on a work implement, perhaps a barrel that was banged by agricultural workers to accompany work songs. My personal theory is that it was devised by the cunning men of Kerry to push up the price of a goatskin.

Above: A bodhran.

Bodhrans are generally circular and covered in animal skins. Usually they are made from goat but they have also been made from donkey, deer, antelope and possibly even dog. Given the fact that wood and animal skins are easily biodegradable, it is unsurprising that no ancient versions have survived. The bodhran does bear an uncanny resemblance to the tray used on farms in Celtic countries for separating chaff from grain. It was Sean Ó Riada who was the first musician to stick his neck out by brazenly describing the bodhran as Ireland's "native drum" and it is through his music that it has become such a popular instrument today.

29

Above: Drumming has always been a part of Irish traditional music.

Above: The Corrs use traditional Irish instruments **30** *to produce a modern and energetic sound appealing to both young and old today.*

Story: Donn Bó

The army of the Leath Chuinn had refused to travel into battle without the presence of their king Ferghal Mac Maelduin's minstrel Donn Bó in order to entertain them. Mac Maelduin appealed to Donn Bó's mother to let her son accompany the army, and she reluctantly agreed. Unfortunately, at the Battle of Almhaine fortune did not favour the brave and both Mac Maelduin and Donn Bó were killed in the battle.

That night, as the victorious men of Leinster were celebrating their victory, their king Murchadh Mac Briain ordered one of his soldiers to fetch him the head of one of the slain enemy on the battlefield. As the servant roamed the battlefield, he heard a voice saying, "You have been commanded by the keening women to play music for your lords tonight". The eerie voice was followed by the harmonious sound of beautiful instruments playing. The source of this magical music was the minstrel Donn Bó's head fulfilling his promise to entertain his king and compatriots that night.

The soldier picked up the head and took it to the king of Leinster's camp but it refused to perform for its captors, it told them, "unless it could face a wall and so avoid the embarrassment of facing my enemy". The sweetness of Donn Bó's lament so overwhelmed the Leinster men that they began to feel ashamed of their slaughter and so they sent a warrior back to the battlefield to fetch the rest of Donn Bó's body in order that they could give it a fine funeral. However, when the body and the head were reunited a strange thing happened: Donn Bó sat up alive and well and made his way home to his mother.

Norman and Medieval Irish Music

The Christian and Monastic Influences

I n the year 432 AD, tradition states, St Patrick landed in Ireland with several loyal followers and spent the rest of his life converting the natives to Christianity. Although the Celtic church of the time did not seek to abolish existing customs, he only altered the natives' beliefs when they were in direct conflict with Christian doctrine.

St Patrick brought with him from Europe the Latin alphabet and in the succeeding years the craft of the written word would be used by Irish monks to record the great wealth of

the country's culture and history. Patrick established monasteries across the country and during the Dark Ages these were to serve as sanctuary to many of continental Europe's scholars and theologians. It was here that the lamp of Latin learning was preserved for all time. It was during this time that the *Book of Kells* and other great illuminated manuscripts of Ireland were created. Many of these are still preserved to this day in Trinity College, Dublin.

During this time, there was a great deal of cross-fertilisation between the Latin and the Celt, particularly in music. The monastic chanting that originated in ancient Judea became mixed with the bardic traditions.

In parts of western Ireland today where Sean Nós singing still survives it is believed that this unique form of modal singing was handed down from the chanting of these monks. The earliest representation of the harp appears in the 9th-century psalter of Folchard, showing the Ark of the Covenant and a crowned King David holding a triangular harp. The psalter was made for the Benedictine monastery of the Irish missionary St Gall who founded the monastery in the early 7th century in Switzerland.

Harps and lyres also feature prominently on high crosses between the 9th and 11th centuries. These carved panels were used as teaching tools for the laity when illuminated books were rare and only a very few people were literate.

During the 9th and 10th centuries the Vikings extensively raided the coast of Ireland and ransacked many of the monasteries. Many books, manuscripts and musical instruments were sadly destroyed. Even when the Vikings had been beaten and Brian Boru had assumed his title of High King, family and clan warfare continued for another one and a half centuries and the only music that was relevant to people during these times was the music played on the war pipes. This was the Age of the Sword.

In 1169, Dermon MacMurrough who was King of Leinster lost his title through conflict. He made an appeal to Henry II, the Plantagenet king of England, for assistance in regaining control. Henry agreed, providing both financial and military support, and thus began a new phase of history for Ireland – the Norman French invasion.

33

Top: Psalter of Folchard.
Above: Henry II.

Court Bards

When the Normans arrived in Ireland in the late 1160s, they began an intensive, artistic renaissance. However, much of the scholarship was due to the ambitions of the local provincial kings. Their druids began compiling new pseudo-histories to endorse claimants in the emerging feudal politics. One of the most dynamic of these was called the *Lebor Gabála Érenn*, which is the *Book of the Taking of Ireland*. This grafted the mythologies of early Ireland onto the story of creation in Genesis. The book connected the aboriginal peoples of Ireland to the descendants of Adam through Japeth. There are other legends connecting the early Irish invaders with the Scythians and also to ancient Egypt.

In the *Lebor Gabála Érenn* there is an account of a feud between Éremon and his kinsman Eber; after judgement was handed down to them by Amergin, their poet and lawmaker, Éremon took the north and Eber the south. They then drew lots for the division of their artists; the poets went north with Éremon and the musicians went south with Eber. This schematic division of the country between the literate north and the musical south was a cunning assertion of artistic and political power.

The Normans themselves did very little to alter the role of the musician at that time. However, the long-term cultural changes brought about by their conquest left a strong imprint on Irish music. The Normans soon began to adopt Irish customs, learning the language and adding Gaelic elements to their surnames. They intermarried with the natives and patronised the musicians. In 1367, the notorious Statutes of Kilkenny were enacted in parliament before Lionel, Duke of Clarence, Lord Lieutenant of Ireland, banning Norman settlers from using Irish laws, language and customs. It also became an offence to entertain the native musicians in case they spied upon Norman secrets. The Gaelic Irish were now required by law to speak English among themselves. After an initial period of oppression the statutes failed and fortunately did little to curb the patronage of musicians.

One of the most significant of musical flowerings was the growth of popularity of the French *amour courtois* or courtly love songs. At this time travelling troubadours made their way across Europe and into Ireland, to entertain at court. The troubadours' themes were those of chivalry and the aforementioned courtly love, although they sang of other subjects as well. The most popular of these love songs were those addressed by the minstrel to a married lover. This was due to the fact that many marriages were arranged and the theme of true love outside of the bonds of marriage, which was usually chaste, struck a chord with the listeners. The most famous of the Irish troubadour poets was known as Gerald the Rhymer whose real name was Gearóid

MacGearailt, the third Earl of Desmond, who was born in 1335. He was also involved on the political scene in both Ireland and France. He took the archaic syllabic verse of the court poets and transformed it into native Irish verse, using the form of the *amhrán* which uses stress metres. His family, known as the Geraldines, eventually abandoned French in favour of the native Irish language as the language of their court. This family played an important part in Irish politics throughout the history of Ireland (such as Edward Fitzgerald). He died in 1398.

During this period, hundreds of noble families were still keeping hereditary *filidh* or bards who were composing in a more modern literary language which came to be called Early Modern Irish.

Sean Nós

Sean Nós, which translates as "old style", is the title given to the oldest surviving form of traditional Irish music. It draws many of its characteristics from medieval bardic poetry. Some of its songs are deemed to date back to the pre-Christian era. Each dialect of Irish has its own special Sean Nós style. What makes Sean Nós different from ordinary singing is that the singer uses the voice box as an instrument and the music is more important than the lyrics themselves. It is always sung a cappella and unaccompanied. The songs stress the lyrical over the narrative and involve a complex system of ornamentation, consisting of rolls, grace notes and the addition of several tones to a syllable. In Sean Nós important notes are lengthened and the glottal stop is frequently used. The singers do not use vibrato and they allow the song to speak for itself. Sean Nós singers do not convey emotion through how loudly or softly they sing but through the ornamentation that they add; how they shape and mould the words and sounds and how much or little they stress the melody and rhythms. The Sean Nós singer also determines their own pace for the song, which seems to take on a life of its own and has its own archaic rituals. The singer often appears to be in a trance, living very much in the moment of artistic reverie and allowing the momentum of the song and its presence to take them over.

A Sean Nós singer will never sing the same song twice in the same way. Aficionados of world music have likened the ornamentation and elaboration of this style to Arabic music. The singers have a very nasal quality to their voices which can give the impression that they are pitching their voices too high. The Connemara Gaeltacht is one of the few places left in Ireland where Sean Nós is still very much a living tradition and in recent decades it has undergone a renaissance.

The Gaeltacht are Irish communities where Gaelic is widely spoken such as Donegal, Mayo, Cork, Kerry and Galway.

Biography: Giraldus Cambrensis

Giraldus Cambrensis was a 12th-century cleric and was one of the first writers to describe Irish music whose records still survive today. His name means Gerald of Wales and indeed he was born in Wales. He was born either in 1146 or 1147 to royal blood; his father was a Norman knight and his mother a Welsh princess. From early on he wished to enter the priesthood, in particular to become Bishop of St David's in Wales, a title which his beloved uncle held.

He travelled widely throughout the continent of Europe, but it is his commentary on Ireland that allows us an early insight into Irish music. In 1167 Giraldus studied in Paris, learning Latin poetry, law, philosophy and theology. He remained there for five years, learning the church songs as well as the secular music from the noble households of England and France.

He wrote 17 books in all; his *Descriptio Cambriae* written on the music of Wales and his *Topographica Hibernica* on the music of Ireland being perhaps the most well known to modern traditional musicians. It was in 1183 that Giraldus made his first visit to Ireland, and he returned two years later with his student Prince John of England. Although he found the Irish to be "barbarians" and criticised their idleness and rural manners, he greatly admired their musical performance skills and the general polyphony found in Irish music.

On the subject of Irish instrumental music, Giraldus has the following to say:

Above: St David's Cathedral, Wales.

36

"I find among these people commendable diligence only on musical instruments, on which they are incomparably more skilled than any nation I have seen. Their style is not, as on the British instruments to which we are accustomed, deliberate and solemn but quick and lively; nevertheless the sound is smooth and pleasant.

It is remarkable that, with such rapid fingerwork, the musical rhythm is maintained and that, by unfailingly disciplined art, the integrity of the tune is fully preserved throughout the ornate rhythms and the profusely intricate polyphony – and with such smooth rapidity, such 'unequal equality', such 'discordant concord'. Whether the strings strike together a fourth or a fifth, the musicians nevertheless always start from B flat and return to the same, so that everything is rounded off in a pleasant general sonority. They introduce and leave rhythmic motifs so subtly, they play the tinkling sounds on the thinner strings above the sustained sound of the thicker string so freely, they take such secret delight and caress the strings so sensuously, that the greatest part of their art seems to lie in veiling it, as if 'that which is concealed is better – art revealed is art shamed'.

Thus it happens that those things which bring private and unequivocal delight to people of subtle appreciation and sharp discernment, burden rather than delight the ears of those who in spite of looking do not see and in spite of hearing do not understand; to unwilling listeners, fastidious things appear tedious and have a confused and disordered sound.

Ireland uses and delights in two instruments only, the cithara (harp) and the tympanum."

(Topographica Hibernica, 1185)

Although he was to obtain the title Archdeacon of Brecon, sadly Giraldus was never to attain the title of Bishop of St David's. He journeyed three times to Rome to ask for the Pope to restore the power of St David's, but he retired to a monastery later in life, having been betrayed by the political intrigue which was going on between crown and church at the time. He continued to write in his old age and died peacefully somewhere between the years 1220 and 1240.

Story: The Satanic Piper

Many hundred years ago when May Eve fell on a Saturday, on the summit of Tops Hill, near the village of Raphoe, a newly married couple with their relatives and friends met at the stone circle there to celebrate their nuptials. Here they feasted and danced merrily until the bell in the nearby church tower tolled midnight and the piper who had been employed by them, being a pious and god-fearing man, refused to play any longer.

The bride, like the guests, being overly fond of dancing, was so exasperated that she swore to her guests that she would find a new piper if she had to go to hell to get one. She had scarcely uttered the words when a venerable old man with long white hair and a long beard made his appearance and proffered his services which were gladly accepted by the surprised company. The suave old gentleman, who was no other than the arch-fiend himself, took the seat vacated by the god-fearing piper, buckled on his instrument and commenced playing a slow and solemn air. This was not the kind of music that his audience wanted to hear, far from it – they wanted to dance and the bride told him so in no uncertain words. Accordingly, and with a knowing smile upon his face, the piper changed his tune and turned his attention to a lively jig and the company began to dance again. They soon found themselves whirling around the demon piper, so fast and furiously that they were more than anxious to take a rest but the more they tried to stop, the faster they found their feet moving and around they whirled, round the diabolical musician who began to change before their very eyes into the horned fiend himself.

Their cries for mercy were unheeded and they danced until daybreak – until they had perspired so greatly that most of the flesh had left their bodies and they had become skeleton-like. As the sun rose over the horizon, the demon stopped his playing. "I leave you now," said the fiend, "a monument of my power and your wickedness until the end of time." And he promptly vanished.

The villagers, on leaving the circle, found the meadows strewn with large pieces of stone and the pious piper lying under a hedge, half dead with fright, having been a witness to the whole scene.

Above: An Irish stone circle.

Tudor and Stuart Times

Henry VIII's Prohibition of Irish Music

By the early 16th century, many Norman families had been assimilated into the Irish way of life. In 1509 Henry VIII, of the Welsh Tudor bloodline, became the King of England. In 1534 Henry summoned the ninth Earl of Kildare to London where he was executed. Later that year the Earl's son, Thomas Fitzgerald led 140 horsemen with silk fringes on their helmets (which led to his nickname of Silken Thomas) to St Mary's Abbey in Dublin in order to publicly renounce their allegiance to Henry. This revolt gave Henry the perfect opportunity to destroy the Geraldine powers in Ireland.

The year 1536 saw Henry VIII break from the Roman Catholic Church in Rome and he then declared himself "Supreme Head on Earth" of both the English and the Irish Church. With the Reformation came the repression of Catholicism and the dissolution of the monasteries. It was in 1541 that Henry also declared himself the King of Ireland.

Both the Catholic monasteries and the Catholic Irish lords were purged of their positions and obliged to accept Tudor laws. Henry VIII realised very quickly that the Irish court musicians had a great deal of political power. In order to maintain control of Ireland he therefore decreed that the bards and their instruments were to be destroyed. A statute in 1533 suppressed the rhymer, the piper and the artistic class in general. Strangely, he found room for Irish pipers within his own military and Irish pipers accompanied his soldiers in his campaign against the Scots and the French.

However, the laws that Henry enacted really only affected an area in the vicinity of Dublin called The Pale, which was the stronghold of the Hiberno-Norman, and therefore Catholic, powerbase. They were designed to ensure the nobility complied with his wishes. Most of the rural areas remained untouched and the peasant classes continued to play whatever they wanted, whenever they wanted. Unfortunately, their tradition was an oral tradition and we have absolutely no written records of the kind of music that they would play at their dances, wakes and other festivals.

Above: King Henry VIII.

40

41

Above: St Mary's Abbey, Dublin.

Conquest of Ireland by Elizabeth I

Elizabeth's conquest of Ireland was the result of a head-on collision between two different civilisations and religious philosophies. England was at that time a Renaissance state and was expanding its colonial interests, whereas Ireland was an oral culture, undergoing political fragmentation. England was under threat from Catholic Spain and Ireland, a strategically useful location to the west of England, could easily have been used as an attack base by the Spanish Armada. Also Elizabethan adventurers were not only imposing their values on the indigenous peoples of the New World but were intent on the same thing in the Gaelic lands.

In order to fulfil her cultural ambitions, Elizabeth sent a new breed of bureaucrats and administrators to colonise Ireland, amongst them celebrated literati such as William Camden and Edmund Spenser. These antiquarians recorded their own impressions of Irish culture and geography. They also found time to comment on the role of music and dancing. Fines Moryson, who was secretary to Lord Mountjoy, left an account of the Irish dancing over naked swords.

Elizabeth passed a number of decrees in an effort to curb the cultural autonomy of the Irish by curtailing the influence of poets and musicians. Towards the end of the Virgin Queen's reign she had extended her power throughout the island through a systematic policy of land confiscation and plantation. Her soldiers had suppressed two rebellions by the Desmonds in 1569 and 1579 that were supported by both Spanish and Italian troops. She also decreed that bards and harpers were to be executed. However, such callous disregard of the role of the bards as custodians of native culture only reinforced the power of music to represent a distinct Gaelic identity.

Ulster remained a political thorn in Elizabeth's side until almost the end of her reign. When the Earl of Essex arrived in 1599, native chieftains such as Hugh O'Neill and Red Hugh O'Donnell presented a definite military challenge. The final confrontation was at the Battle of Kinsale in 1601 when O'Donnell and O'Neill, along with their Spanish allies, were heavily defeated by the Elizabethan army. This crushing defeat of the Ulster chieftains is

Above: Queen Elizabeth I.

still remembered in the Munster air called "The Lament for O'Donnell". The Battle of Kinsale itself was a watershed in both Irish musical and literary history. Within the next century, 85 per cent of the land was transferred to the new English colonists and the Irish system of artistic patronage had vanished forever.

Elizabeth I died in 1603 and was followed by the Stuart bloodline of Scotland, firstly James I (1566–1625) and then his son Charles I (1600–1649).

The Ulster Plantation Music

In 1607, 90 Ulster chieftains went into voluntary exile to the Catholic European mainland, including O'Neill and O'Donnell. They took with them their retinues of poets and musicians. The "Flight of the Earls" deprived the remaining bards of patronage who instead became itinerant musicians.

In December 1607 the departed lords had their lands confiscated. Sir Arthur Chichester masterminded the plantation of Ulster and drove thousands of native Irish people off 500,000 prime acres of land in Tyrone, Derry, Antrim and Armagh. The province was resettled by Presbyterian Gaelic-speaking lowland Scots from Galloway and Argyle and although the plantation nurtured the seeds of sectarian bitterness, the repercussions of which are still felt today, it introduced new music and musicians into Ireland.

The Ulster Scots had a predilection for the fife and drum but also brought jigs and weavers' ballads with them. Their anglicised culture also helped the dispersal of ballad sheets which contained popular English and Scottish ballads.

In 1641, the first revolt against the Stuart regime took place in Ireland, led by a group of rebels known as the Confederation of Kilkenny. There are contemporary records referring to bagpipers serving in the Confederate forces during this rebellion. The most famous piping tune to survive was called "Alasdruim's March", composed in memory of Alasdair Mac Colla who was killed at the Battle of Cnoc Nan Dos in County Cork in 1647. The march ends with a series of laments for the slain soldier.

Cromwell's Resettlement

After Charles I was executed in 1649, the puritanical zealot Oliver Cromwell took over the running of England as Lord Protector and also ordered the subjugation of Ireland. Cromwell landed in Dublin that same year at the head of a Puritan army, determined to crush the Royalist and Catholic cause in Ireland. His vicious slaughter of both soldiers and civilians in the garrison towns of Drogheda and Wexford has left an indelible imprint and is still remembered in songs. His brutal resettlement also transformed the land-owning aristocracy by removing the distinctions between the native Irish and the old English. The leaders of the rebellion, who were both old English and native Irish Catholics, forfeited all land and property rights to the Commonwealth. Catholic priests were outlawed and those who remained active rebels risked being summarily hanged or transported to the West Indies. Musicians, too, were were exported to the West Indies by Cromwell and there sold into slavery or indentured service.

Following in the footsteps of the Flight of the Earls, many Irish soldiers fled into voluntary exile into Europe and joined Irish regiments within other European armies. One such hero, Colonel Edmund O'Dwyer, leader of the Munster forces, left Ireland with some 4,500 of his men after they had surrendered to the Cromwellian army at Cahir, County Tipperary, in 1652.

Above: Oliver Cromwell 1599–1658.

44

The restoration of the English monarchy in 1660 under Charles II did very little to stop Cromwell's confiscations. Charles did suspend the penal laws against Catholics and non-conformist Protestants in 1672, but Parliament forced him to withdraw his Declaration of Indulgence the following year. His son James II acceded to the throne in 1685 but his pro-Catholic stance drove the British Parliament to bring William of Orange over from Holland to replace him as monarch.

The Williamite Wars and their Music

Ireland raised an army in favour of James, who arrived in Cork in March 1689 to the sounds of bagpipers and dancing. The tune "Lilli Bulero", which eventually became the

Above: Drogheda.

signature tune of Custer's Fifth Cavalry, in America, was reputedly played on this occasion. In June 1690 William of Orange landed in Carrick Fergus in County Antrim and the two armies met at the River Boyne on 1 July 1690. William's army consisted of 36,000 men, mainly Germans, Dutch, Danes and French Protestants, whereas James Stuart's army of 24,000 was made up of French and Irish Catholic troops. After a day of fighting, James fled the battlefield and escaped to France. William's army emerged from the slaughter victorious and inspired the huge repertoire of mainland Europe Protestant marching tunes which are still played in Ulster today. After the Battle of the Boyne, the Jacobite generals withdrew to the River Shannon and their final stand was during the first siege of Limerick. General Patrick Sarsfield held Limerick against a fierce Williamite onslaught. William of Orange eventually returned to

England, leaving the Dutch General Ginkel in charge. Ginkel was to cross the Shannon and the Battle of Aughrim ensued. This military encounter, remembered by poets and musicians as "Aughrim's Dread Disaster" was captured in the battle lament "The Crying of the Women in the Slaughter".

After the second siege of Limerick, a treaty was agreed, allowing General Sarsfield and 14,000 men to go to France where they joined the army of Louis XIV and became known as the Wild Geese. Their departure inspired the lament called "Lament of Limerick" and their regimental valour on the battlefields of Europe was immortalised in the song "Clare's Dragoons".

Above: William of Orange and a mural of his landing in Carrick Fergus, County Antrim.

Clare's Dragoons

By Thomas Osbourne Davis

When on Ramilles´ bloody field
The baffled French were forced to yield,
The victor Saxon backward reeled
Before the charge of Clare´s Dragoons.
The flags we conquered in that fray
Look lone in Ypres choir they say.
We´ll win them company today,
Or bravely die like Clare´s Dragoons.

Viva la, for Ireland´s wrong!
Viva la, for Ireland´s right!
Viva la, in battle throng,
For a Spanish steed and a sabre bright!

The brave old lord died near the fight,
But for each drop he lost that night
A Saxon cavalier shall bite
The dust, before Lord Clare´s Dragoons.
For never, when our spurs were set,
And never, when our sabres met,
Could we the Saxon soldiers get
To stand the shock of Clare´s Dragoons.

Viva la, the New Brigade!
Viva la, the old one too!
Viva la, the Rose shall fade
And the Shamrock shine for ever new!

O comrades! Think how Ireland pines,
Her exiled lords, her rifled shrines,
Her dearest hope the ordered lines
And bursting charge of Clare´s Dragoons.
Then fling the Green Flag to the sky,
And "Limerick!" be your battle cry,
And charge till blood flows fetlock-high
Around the track of Clare´s Dragoons!

47

The success of William of Orange left 90 per cent of the land of Ireland in Protestant hands. The Parliament there was also entirely Protestant; Catholics were forced to pay tithes to the Anglican church and a whole series of anti-Catholic penal measures were placed on the statute books. Although laws had been enacted penalising religious minorities throughout Europe since the Reformation, the Irish penal laws were unusual because they were directed against the majority. For example, Catholics were excluded from Parliament, the legal profession, government services, teaching and the army. It was illegal for Catholics to bear arms, to own a horse worth more than five pounds or to send their children to Europe to be educated, and they were not allowed to purchase land. In 1697 the Irish Parliament passed an act banishing Catholic bishops and monks, as well as regular clergy. Under these circumstances, going to mass was dangerous and became an underground movement inspiring many songs. In fact many Catholic masses, including weddings, were held out in the open in the old stone circles of the pagans.

Although there was a hundred years of peace following the Williamite wars, most of the population lived in abject poverty, with the exception of north-east Ulster which had a thriving linen industry, under the direction of French Protestant refugees who had been banished from Catholic France. The last remnants of the bardic order managed to survive by obtaining patronage from the new Protestant landlords and were obliged to compromise some of their musical pieces with English and continental styles, although others did retain the archaic style of Irish harping by continuing to play with long fingernails on wire-strung harps.

The itinerant harpers' lifestyle was harsh. They travelled the length and breadth of Ireland, relying entirely on the generosity of their patrons for their livelihood. Many were blind and depended on a guide to lead them. In 1730 the first Convention of the Bards was held in Brewery, County Limerick, in order to preserve the oral art of the harper. A number of harp festivals helped to create support for the harpers and fostered public awareness of their plight.

Laments

Laments are the oldest form of song surviving in Ireland. Many of the earlier ones are religious laments to the Virgin Mary called *Amhráin Bheannaithe*, which translate as "religious songs". They include the lament of "The Three Marys" and "The Lament of the Virgin". There are also funeral and death laments, the most common being the keen, performed by the *Bhean Chaointe* (chanting women) around the body. This keening or chanting was a communal process that acted as a form of collective catharsis. The second type was the *Marbhna* or bardic elegy which was composed by the patronised *filidh* for his dead chieftain in syllabic metre. The third type of death lament became popular after the decline of the bardic schools and was a type of *Marbhna* composed in stress metre by poets who wished to prolong the traditions of the bards. The fourth was the simple death song which still features in the Sean Nós (old style) songs of Donegal. These songs are usually about tragedies and disasters but are not sung at wakes or funerals.

The Fenian Lays

The Fenian Lays were ballads based on mythological adventures of Fionn Mac Cumhail (Finn McCool). The stories were set down originally as poetry and were then sung at court assemblies and communal gatherings. These lays (*laoithe*) were based on the *Agallamh na Seanorach*, a 12th-century prose compilation known as the "Old Men's Discourse". In this story Oisín returns from Tír Na Nóg (the Land of Youth) and joins St Patrick on his mission around Ireland and recites tales to him about the places they visit.

The mythological hero Fionn Mac Cumhail was the leader of the Fianna, an army maintained by Cormac Mac Airt, the High King in Tara. These lays were usually sung in four-line verses and were full of magical encounters, journeys to the land of youth, battles with monsters and elopements with forbidden beauties. During Tudor and Stuart times these lays were sung by all classes of society throughout the whole Gaelic world. This tradition has survived amongst the Gaelic singers and storytellers and the tales of Finn McCool, the giant who built the Giant's Causeway, and his wife Oona, are still told around firesides today.

Above: The Giant's Causeway – reputed to have been built by Finn McCool.

"My eyes have been transplanted into my ears"
Turlough O'Carolan

Turlough O'Carolan

Turlough O'Carolan (Toirdhealbhach Ó Cearbhallain) was born in 1670, near Nobber in County Meath. He was known as one of the last Irish harpers to compose and his gift was to leave behind an incredible legacy of poetry and music, including 200 airs which have immortalised his fame.

In the 1680s his family moved to Ballyfarnon and it was there he met Mrs MacDermott of the MacDermott Roe family. She was to take him under her wing and gave him an education, through which he showed a talent for poetry. He first studied the harp in 1688; sadly this was the year he contracted smallpox which left him blind in both eyes. However, he was to continue with his studies and in 1691 he completed his apprenticeship and composed his first tune "Sheebeg and Sheemore". At the end of his studying Mrs MacDermott gave him his own harp, a horse and money in order that he could make a living as a harper.

O'Carolan would travel, mainly in County Connacht, between patrons. His presence at the grand houses was regarded as a great honour to the inhabitants within. He instinctively understood that hospitality had its limitations and was careful to move on in his wanderings, but on many occasions was pressed to prolong his stay. He once replied to a gentleman urging him to stay: "If to a friend's house thou shouldst repair; pause and take heed of lingering idly there; thou mayest be welcome but it's past a doubt; long visits soon will wear the welcome out."

He would write the music first and then the words. His emphasis was always on the poetry with the tune as accompaniment which was contrary to normal Irish practice. He would also add elements of European music of the time such as Vivaldi as well as combining the art music and folk music traditions within the context of the harper tradition.

The tunes he wrote were usually dedicated to a patron, such as Dr John Hart, Bishop of Achonry or Colonel John Irwin.

Little is known of O'Carolan's family. However, he did marry a Mary Maguire and had seven children, one of whom, his only son, was to publish his father's tunes in the late 1740s. O'Carolan's surviving melodies appear only as one-liners with no information on how they were accompanied or harmonised as he originally intended them to be heard.

It is easy to hear the influence of the fairies in O'Carolan's compositions, such as "The Fairy Queen", as he used to get his inspiration from a nearby fairy rath (mound), but he was also known to imbibe large quantities of alcohol on a regular basis. There are many tales of his drunken exploits and, although he was told to quit drinking for health reasons, he was so addicted that it made him more ill to stop.

In 1733 his wife died and five years later O'Carolan died at the home of his first patron Mrs MacDermott. He received a four-day wake in his honour which was attended by many.

Above: Turlough O'Carolan.

Story: The Petrified Piper

Once upon a time, on a dark and moonless night, Remmy Carroll, the renowned piper, and Pat Minahan, the voracious chronicler, were walking along the soft path at the foot of the mountain of Corran Thierna. Remmy suddenly stopped and exclaimed, "There's music somewhere about here!"

"Maybe 'tis only singing in your head," observed Minahan. "I've known such things, especially if one had been taking a drop extra."

"Hush!" said Remmy. "I hear it again as distinctly as I ever heard the sound of me own pipes; hush now, there it is again."

Pat paused and listened: "Sure enough now, there is music in the air."

"Oh! Remmy, 'tis you are a lucky boy for this must be fairy music and 'tis said that whoever hears it as you did is surely born to good luck."

"Never mind the luck," said Remmy laughing. "There's the fairy ring above us and I'll be bound that's the place the music is coming from."

"Maybe it does and maybe it doesn't," replied Pat, "and if you please I'd rather move on for it seems to be getting darker and darker here. 'Twas somewhere about here that Phil Connor,

the piper, had a trial of skill with the fairies and they turned him into a stone, pipes and all, did you ever hear of that?"

Remmy said that he had not but that if he had he would not have believed it.

"Well then," continued his companion, nodding his head wisely, "'tis all as true as that you are alive this minute. I heard it from a mother and she got it from a cousin who had the story from a good authority. Phil Connor was a piper and a mighty fine player entirely and one fine moonlit night he was coming home from a wedding at Rath Cormac and who should come tripping along the same mountainside but a whole troupe of fairies a-singing, and a-skipping and a-talking and as civil as you please they upped and asked him if he would favour them with a tune upon his pipes. Now, letting alone that Phil was as courageous as a dog and would not even mind facing an angry woman, not to mention a lot of weenie hop-on-my-thumb fairies, he did not have the heart to say no, especially when he was so civilly approached. So he struck up the old tune 'The Foxhunter's Jig' and sure as I'm telling you, no one could play it better than he. The moment the fairies heard it they all began to caper and dance backwards and forwards, to and fro like midges of an evening in summer. Then Phil stopped suddenly and they all gathered around him to find out what was the matter. The piper told them that he must have something to wet his whistle as his mouth was dry as a bone. "To be sure," said a gnarled old fairy, "that's only reasonable, bring the gorsoon a drink of something good." And so they handed a fairy finger full of a drink that had a mighty pleasant smell and they filled a cup of the same for the gnarled old fairy, who it seemed was their king. "And here's to you, my fine piper," says he, "there's not a headache in a hogshead of it I warrant ye and it was made in Araglin of mountain barley." And with that he drank to Phil and Phil raised the little thimble-sized cup to his mouth and thought it was not more than a dram but he drank at least a half a pint of it and when he finished it was still full to the brim. The drink gave the piper the boldness of a lion and the foolishness of a babe and what he did was to challenge the whole of them to equal him in the playing of the pipes. Although some of them well advised him to keep quiet, the more they persuaded the more he insisted and at long last the fairies' piper came forward and took up the challenge and so at it they went, Phil Connor and the fairy piper playing against each other until the cock crowed. Then the whole gang vanished into a cave in the hillside, taking along the brave Phil with them, pipes and all, but that was not the end of it. They were so downright mad because their fairy piper could not get the best of Phil that they changed him into a stone statue which remains in the cave to this day and that is what happened to Phil Connor, the piper, for daring to offend the good people."

55 *Above: The drink gave the piper the boldness of a lion and the foolishness of a babe and what he did was to challenge the whole of them to equal him in the playing of the pipes.*

Pre-Famine Irish Music

The Belfast Harpers' Festival

O n 11–13 July 1792 the first Belfast Harpers' Festival took place in Belfast's Exchange Rooms. The festival had been organised by a number of prominent Belfast citizens including Dr James MacDonnell, Thomas Russell and Henry Joy McCracken. An array of monetary prizes was offered and ten Irish harpers attended. They included Denis Hempson from Derry, age 97; Arthur O'Neill from Tyrone, age 58; Daniel Black from Derry, age 75; Hugh Higgins of Mayo, age 75; Patrick Quin of Armagh, age 47; and Rose Mooney from Meath, age 52, all of whom were blind. Also attending were Charles Fanning from Cavan, age 56; Charles Byrne of Leitrim, age 80; William Carr of Armagh, age 15; and James Duncan of County Down, age 45. There was also a Welsh harper called Williams.

Above: The Belfast Harpers' Festival.

Denis Hempson

Of the ten harpers who competed at the Belfast Harpers' Festival, Denis Hempson, or O'Hempsey, at 97 years old was the only harper who played his harp with long fingernails as harpers from the old times did. Hempson was born in 1695 at Craighmore, near Garvagh, Derry. He contracted smallpox at the age of three which resulted in him losing his eyesight. At the age of 12 he began to study the harp under the tuition of Bridget O'Cahan. In those days both women and men in the best families were taught harp. He then studied under John C Garragher, who was also blind, and a succession of other travelling harpers from Connacht. In his youth he knew Turlough O'Carolan.

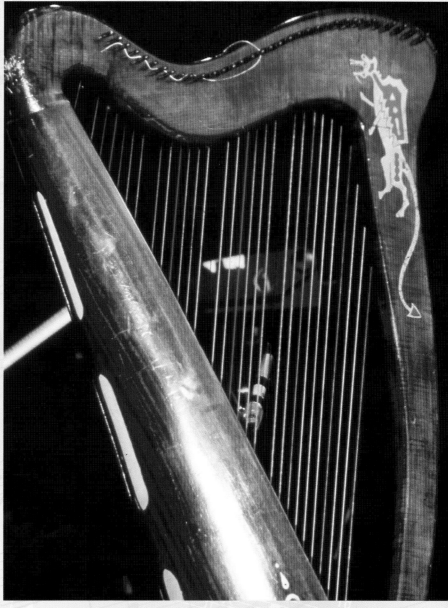

At 18 he was given his own harp by three of the worthies from his home town. Over the next ten years he toured Ireland and Scotland. In 1745 he played before Bonnie Prince Charlie in Edinburgh. For the rest of his career he played in the houses of the nobility and gentry throughout Ireland. Like all travelling musicians he was a great conversationalist, full of stories and anecdotes about his travels.

When he was 86 he married a woman at Magilligan in Derry and they had a daughter together, with whom he spent the last years of life. He died at home at the astounding age of 112, with his favourite harp in his hands.

The Bard Of Armagh (Traditional)

Oh, list to the lay of a poor Irish harper
And scorn not the strains of his old withered hand,
But remember his fingers they once could move sharper
To raise up the memory of his dear native land.

At a fair or a wake I could twist my shillelagh
Or trip through a jig with my brogues bound with straw
And all the pretty colleens in the village or the valley
Loved their bold Phelim Brady, the bard of Armagh.

Oh, how I long to muse on the days of my boyhood
Though four-score and three years have flitted since then,
But it bring sweet reflections as every young joy should
For the merry-hearted boys make the best of old men.

And when Sergeant Death in his cold arms shall embrace me
Then lull me to sleep with sweet Erin go Bragh,
By the side of my Kathleen, my young wife, then place me
And forget Phelim Brady, the bard of Armagh.

Rural Music

Rural Ireland during the early 1800s was composed of clusters of farmhouses and communities of families, connected through close ties of kinship and called *clachán*. In these communities the diet consisted mostly of potatoes which had been introduced from the New World centuries earlier in the plantations. Nearly three-quarters of the Irish population formed these clacháns. The music-making in the clacháns followed the pattern of the agricultural year, that is sowing, harvesting, potato digging etc. When work was done the neighbours and kin groups congregated in the clachán kitchens where completion of the work was celebrated with music, dancing and food. There were also race meetings, fairs, hurling matches, weddings, funerals and baptisms as well as patron saints' days. All of these were celebrated to the full.

Itinerant pipers enjoyed high status at these gatherings; they were carriers of news as well as entertainment. Their arrival always prompted a *ragairne* which is a house dance. The pipers followed well-known routes and dates around the country which were planned around the working year of their patrons. The blind pipers, of which there were many, usually travelled with a child from place to place. The Sean Nós singers in these communities sang love songs, work and religious songs, laments, lullabies, satires and children's recreational songs. The most popular genre, however, was songs of the supernatural. Fairy lore was and still is particularly popular in Irish-speaking communities and these songs recounted tales of abductions, changelings and musical exchanges with the fairy folk.

Set Dances

At this time there was a great deal of traffic between Ireland and the European mainland, including smuggling. This traffic naturally brought cultural influences for musicians and dancers. The model violin which traditional musicians renamed the fiddle was introduced, as were a whole group of new dances. The Rince Fada was a popular group dance in Ireland which was a combination of dancing and marching. It was danced in jig time, usually on May Eve. The group would pick a King and a Queen, usually the two best dancers, who were given the task of carrying the May Eve garland and hailing the return of summer with the song "Thugamar Féin an Samhradh Linn" (We brought the summer with us). The Rince Fada was danced at the end of private and public balls amongst the gentry. There was also a dance called the Cake Dance in which a cake was offered to the best dancing couple. There were planting dances and sword dances, too, amongst others.

It was not only dances that were brought in; dancing masters came with them. These travelled throughout the country with a piper or a fiddler. They taught jigs, minuets and cotillions – reels and hornpipes did not arrive until the end of the 19th century when they were introduced from Scotland and England respectively. The dancing masters were flamboyant and egocentric characters who considered themselves to be gentlemen. They also taught fencing and deportment to children of the gentry and when they arrived in a village or rural clachán they were greatly welcomed. The reputation of a dancing master rested not only on their ability to teach but also on their talent for inventing new dances, particularly solo ones which would be performed on a small impromptu stage.

Above: Dancing masters travelled throughout the country with a piper or a fiddler.

During the Napoleonic Wars, quadrilles were introduced into Ireland by returning soldiers. They became so popular that even the Knight of Glin in West Limerick gave orders that dancing masters within his domain were to teach these new dances. There were various adaptations of quadrille figures during the early 1800s: the Lancers, the Plain Set and the Caledonian, the Orange and the Green, the Paris Set and the Televara.

61 *Above: An Irish dancing competition in the 1930s. Dancing traditions have lived on down the ages and adapted to suit the times and social changes, appealing to all ages, even today.*

Edward Bunting

Edward Bunting was chosen to write down the notes of the tunes played at the first Belfast Harpers' Festival in 1792. He was born in Armagh in 1773. His grandfather was a piper by the name of Quinn and his father was an Englishman who came to Ireland to open a coal mine in Tyrone. Edward was one of three brothers, all of whom studied music at Armagh and became professional organists.

During his youth his mother's family immersed him in traditional Irish music. Such was his musical genius that it was not long until he was teaching pupils older than himself. Not only did he excel in music, he mastered the skill to tune and repair the instruments. He was recognised as a prodigy and it was at the age of 19 that he was selected to transcribe at the Belfast Harpers' Festival. For the next four years he devoted himself to the work of collecting airs. Bunting travelled all around Ireland, meeting many musicians in the rural areas and, at the same time, he visited the many country houses and met other collectors of music.

In 1796 Bunting produced his first volume which contained 66 native Irish airs that had never been published before. Unfortunately, cheap editions of his publication were bootlegged and he was to go largely unrewarded for the work that he had put into his collection. He continued to collect and research traditional Irish music during the intervals of his occupation as organist and teacher. In 1809 he published his second volume called *A General Collection of the Ancient Music of Ireland, arranged for the pianoforte and voice*. It also contained a historical and critical dissertation on the harp. The 77 airs that he collected had English verses by Thomas Campbell, Miss Balfour and others set to the tunes. As his years advanced, so Bunting's fame increased and his company was sought in the best society of the time. He formed many acquaintances with distinguished men within his profession.

In 1840 Bunting published his third volume which bore the title *The Ancient Music of Ireland* and this contained over 100 airs and

Above: Edward Bunting.

musical examples. It also contained valuable insights relating to the characteristics of Irish melodies and included sketches of famous Irish pipers amongst other articles.

The work gained critical acclaim, not just in Ireland but in England too. He died on 21 December 1843.

Above; An Irish piper .

Story: The Silent Piper

Way back in the year 1840, Mickey O'Donovan's daughter Biddy was to be married to Morty Maguire and by a peculiar combination of circumstances neither a piper nor a fiddler was available to play at their wedding. However, on the day of the wedding a strange and unknown piper entered the village. He was a thin, plaintive-looking old man, much bent by age, and being stone blind he was led by a pretty golden-haired little maiden with a blue ribbon in her hair and glittery beads. His opportune appearance was hailed with delight by every member of both families for he carried his welcome with him in the bagpipes under his arm.

"What could you play sir if you please?" questioned pretty Biddy Donovan, the bride-to-be.

"'Haste to the Wedding' or whatever you please, Miss," answered the golden-haired girl shyly.

"But why can't your father answer for himself?" asked Biddy.

"If you please, Miss, it's a vow that's upon him for his own reason," replied the child, "and so I myself am his tongue as well as his eyes, Miss."

"Oh indeed! Poor man! See that now! A vow! Sin is a shocking thing!" were the exclamations from the relatives.

"'Tis no sin of his own," said the child, "but one that he took upon himself for one that he loved."

Now the Irish are a very inquisitive people and after the strangers had been warmed and fed, and everyone who could dance had taken a turn to the melodious piping of the old man, artful questioning elicited from the child information that the blind piper was her father and it was her mother, when she lay dying, that left the vow upon him. He had never spoken since. She would not say where they came from and she would not say where they were going. Kelly the local piper, whose instrument was being repaired, was obliged to confess on the wedding day that he could not hold a candle to the music of the silent piper. One or two of the very old people hinted that something was not right for they had heard the great pipers in their youth, but never as melodious and sweet as the newcomer played. The fame of the silent piper eventually reached the houses of the gentry and all who heard him were charmed by his wonderful performance. A cottage and a garden were even offered to him with the promise that all his needs would be supplied if only he would settle in the neighbourhood. In reply he only shook his head and sighed and the little maid, with tears in her eyes, told them that they rarely stayed more than a week in any one place.

Now obligations or vows were not uncommon amongst the Irish peasantry but no-one had ever heard of a circumstance like this. And so they both accepted the gifts that were thrust upon them and the old man played O'Carolan's "Lament" to signal that he was about to leave and there were many wet eyes in his audience.

Many years afterwards, while visiting the ancient and picturesque town of Kinsale, Biddy Maguire heard the sound of a bagpipe and followed it to be nearer the player. There, after a lapse of nearly 20 years, sat the silent piper with the very same child at his knee. He played again the bold brave notes of "Brian Boru's March" and as always the women stamped their feet to the tune and when he finished, Biddy Maguire then questioned the young girl as to her memories of Bannow, County Wexford, where her wedding had been held all that time ago.

"Yes dear," answered the old man much to Biddy's surprise, "I do remember Bannow and I remember you too."

"And what about you?" Biddy asked the girl.

"Well, I've never been there, marm," she answered. And yet she wore the same bead

necklace that glittered in the sun and the same blue ribbon was plaited in her hair.

Hearing Biddy's consternation at the answer, the old piper explained, "Ah, my dear lady, that was her mother, bless her, her own mother, my daughter Kathleen who is the mother of a family now."

While Biddy was smiling at her own absurdity the original Kathleen made her appearance, a stout, gleeful woman with a child in her arms and yet another standing at her side. She explained that her father had promised her mother that he would not speak again until their daughter was a married woman herself.

Above: The Blind Piper.

Irish Music During the 1800s

The Great Famine

In 1841 the census in Ireland revealed a population of over 8 million, the majority of whom lived below subsistence levels, particularly in the western areas like County Clare. Areas like this housed several hundred people per square mile of arable land and were the most heavily populated in Europe. However, the population could be supported as long as they had an adequate supply of potato, their staple diet. One rupture in the food cycle could throw the whole system out – and the rupture came in the form of *phytophthora infestans*, a mould and plant pathogen first identified in Flanders, Belgium, whose spores were carried in the wind. It reached Ireland late in the summer of 1845 and the country's damp climate helped to propagate it.

The resulting famine lasted for four years; it caused devastation and changed the face of Ireland and therefore Irish music as we know it today. In the 10-year period 1845–1855 Ireland's population declined from 8.5 million to just under 6 million. The famine began with a blight of the potato crop that left acres of Irish farmland covered with black rot. Subsistence-level Irish farmers, who relied almost solely on the potato for both their diet and the rent that they paid to their landlords, found that the potatoes that they had stored in their cellars were rotten. With no money to buy coffins the dead lay unburied, which led to further outbreaks of diseases such as typhus and cholera. Landlords evicted hundreds of thousands of peasants who were unable to pay their rent, who then crowded into disease-infested workhouses. Other landlords paid for their tenants to emigrate, sending hundreds of thousands of Irish people to America and other English-speaking countries. In many cases these ships reached port having lost over a third of their passengers to disease and hunger.

Above: The Irish potatoe famine is the subject of this modern-day mural.

The famine changed centuries-old agricultural practices, hastening the division of family estates into tiny lots, only capable of sustaining life with potato crops. Although Irish nationalism was dormant for the first half of the 19th century, the famine convinced both Irish citizens and Irish-Americans of the urgent need for political change. In the decade that followed the Great Famine almost 30 per cent of the population emigrated.

This tragic disaster had a devastating effect on the tradition of the work song. As land use changed over from small tillage plots to pasture land, the demand for agricultural labour decreased. The traditional songs associated with ploughing, reaping and sowing declined and disappeared from the oral tradition.

Thousands of musicians were affected by the famine and its diaspora. Many died and even more followed their audiences into exile. Many pipers, fiddlers and dancing masters ended their days in the workhouse and a great silence fell on the land of song.

67

Above: A caricature depicting the Irish potato famine and the plight of the people of Ireland.

Loss of Language and Tradition

Another effect of the Great Famine was the decline of the Irish language, particularly in the western parts of Ireland. This decline undermined much of the folklore and superstitions that sustained the music-makers and songsters. New anglicised place names began to take over from the Gaelic, and the place name lore associated with many of the tunes failed to translate into the English language.

Songs appeared in English which offered another perspective on the famine such as songs of emigration, the reality of overcrowded workhouses, quicklime burials, exile and loneliness. Many of these songs were, of course, composed in the United States. As the economic pressure on landlords increased, mass evictions were normal.

IRISH SKETCHES—COTTAGERS AT KILDARE

Above: Life in rural Ireland became increasingly hard. The old world of the clachán with its gatherings of travelling pipers, folk poets, dancing masters and agricultural festivals was now seen as morally suspect.

68

Collectors of Music

Life in rural Ireland was changed forever and became increasingly hard and materialistic. The old world of the clachán with its gatherings of travelling pipers, folk poets, dancing masters and agricultural festivals was now seen as morally suspect. The Catholic church initiated a new evangelical mission throughout the countryside and the priest became not only a moral arbiter but a social one as well.

During the 1870s a war to secure tenants' rights and ownership began. It was known as the Land War. Marching bands were formed to parade at rallies and meetings.

There had already been a long tradition of marching bands in the political movements of Ireland since the Orange fife and drum bands in the early 1700s. By the end of the 19th century most rural areas had fife and drum bands that played at rallies and religious meetings. Some of these bands were actually trained by British army bandmasters stationed in garrison towns. The bands were responsible for the changeover from the oral tradition of musical conveyance to musical literacy and many musicians played in a fife and drum band during the day and at the country houses during the evening. It was during this time that the concertina arrived in Ireland and became a common household object, particularly in western Ireland. The concertina replaced the pipes as instrument of choice, particularly amongst women.

It was only natural after the great diaspora of musicians following the famine that there was fear that the oral musical tradition would disappear completely and so the Society for the Preservation and Publication of the Melodies of Ireland was founded by the antiquarian George Petrie in 1851. Petrie himself had already travelled around Ireland during the 1830s indexing historical monuments and place names for the Ordnance Survey Commission. During this time he met many traditional musicians in the rural areas.

The Society hoped to create a music archive in Dublin that other music collectors throughout the country could contribute to. Although these ambitions were never realised the Society did publish Petrie's *Ancient Music of Ireland* in 1855.

John Edward Pigot reputedly had over 3,000 unpublished pieces of music in his collection and Dr Henry Hudson of Dublin had 870 tunes, 137 of which were transcribed from Patrick Connelly, who was a blind Galway piper.

The Reverend James Goodman was a musically literate piper who spoke fluent Irish. After graduating from Trinity College, Dublin, he eventually became Professor of Irish there in 1844, and compiled four volumes of traditional music between 1860 and 1866.

69

71   *Above: Traditional musicians playing at an Irish
dancing competition in 1937.*

Biography: Dr Patrick Weston Joyce

Another collector, Patrick Weston Joyce of Limerick, began collecting in the 1850s at the suggestion of Petrie who was indebted to Joyce for many of the airs that he himself published. Joyce's first book, published in 1869, was *Irish Names of Places*. He then published *Ancient Irish Music* in 1873 following the death of Petrie in 1866, *Irish Music and Song* in 1886 and finally a collection called *Old Irish Folk Music and Songs* in 1909.

Joyce was born in 1827 in Ballyorgan, into a household which revered the traditions of Ireland. He learned fiddle from an early age and spent his time mixing with the local peasantry. The preface to his book *Ancient Irish Music* says that he "loved the graceful music of the people from my childhood; their songs, dance tunes, keens and lullabies, remained on my memory almost without any effort of my own ... when my own memory was exhausted, I went among the peasantry during vacations for several successive years, noting down whatever I thought worthy of preserving, both music and words".

Patrick Joyce died in 1914.

Joyce's brother Robert was also a prolific publisher and collector. He published articles with strong Irish nationalist themes. He was a supporter of Fenianism and his ballads are infused with a strong sense of patriotism. Following his graduation as a doctor, Robert Joyce emigrated to America where he built up a large medical practice. He returned to Ireland in 1883 and died in his brother's home. One of his best-known songs is "The Boys of Wexford".

Celtic Revivals

In 1893 the Gaelic League, Conradh Na Gaeilge, was established by Douglas Hyde and Eion McNeill. The League focused on the Irish language and the reconstruction of Irish music, song and dance. The movement quickly spread throughout Ireland as well as to Irish immigrant communities in England and the United States. They held their first *céilí* in London in 1897, laid down rules for dancing and began organising music and singing competitions. The spontaneous set dancing of rural Ireland was quite different from the formal dances of the Gaelic League *céilí* where Victorian decorum and good taste were observed. Although urban Ireland enjoyed its cultural renaissance, the traditional rural musicians and dancers were quite indifferent to it. By the early 1900s some nationalists even believed that its formal set dancing was foreign and, therefore, improper.

The country house musicians at this time, who had no contact with the urban literati, still followed the work cycle of the agricultural workers and played at the ritual

gatherings. Much of their music was played at "American wakes" which were dances held for departing emigrants at which they were fêted by friends and family. During this time Irish traditional music began to

identify more with the Irish music scene in America than with its own middle-class literate scene in the cities of Ireland. More and more of the musicians themselves began to emigrate.

73

Above: The country house musicians at this time, who had no contact with the urban literati, still followed the work cycle of the agricultural workers and played at the ritual gatherings.

The Holy Ground (Traditional)

Fare thee well my lovely Dinah, a thousand times adieu,
For we're going away from the Holy Ground and the girls we all love true.
We will sail the salt sea over and then return for sure
To see again the girls we love and the Holy Ground once more.

Fine girl you are!
You're the girl I do adore
and still I live in hopes to see the Holy Ground once more.
Fine girl you are!

And now the storm is raging and we are far from shore
And the good old ship is tossing about and the riggin' is all tore
And the secret of my mind, my love, you're the girl I do adore
And still I live in hopes to see the Holy Ground once more.

Fine girl you are!
You're the girl I do adore
and still I live in hopes to see the Holy Ground once more.
Fine girl you are!

And now the storm is over and we are safe and well
We will go into a Public House and we'll sit and drink like hell.
We will drink strong ale and porter and we'll make the rafters roar
And when our money is all spent we'll go to sea once more.

Fine girl you are!
You're the girl I do adore
and still I live in hopes to see the Holy Ground once more.

Story: The Dun Hallow Piper

A long time ago and only last year on a cold November morning, Daniel O'Leary, the best piper in Munster, was roused from his bed at his sister's house in the town of Millstreet. The previous night, he had been engaged playing for a party of gentlemen that dined at the Wallace Arms. He had scarcely put his head upon the pillow when his repose was interrupted. It was a message from the Squire of Kilmeen commanding his attendance at his castle. He was throwing a grand party and, though a fiddler or two had been hired, Miss Julia Twomey, one of the young ladies invited, could abide no other music than Daniel O'Leary's.

Although Daniel had no relish for the interruption of much needed rest, he had too much respect for the Squire to disregard his summons. He was just about to mount the fine horse which the Squire had sent for him, when a blue-eyed maiden from Knocknagrue, who was an old sweetheart of Daniel's, passed by. Daniel directed the Squire's messenger to walk the horse slowly on before them while he and Nancy Walsh went into the public house by the crossroads. There they were so agreeably entranced with each other's company over a few glasses of punch that it was dark before they parted. And so, after taking a parting kiss, the piper hurried on his way, hoping to overtake the Squire's messenger with the horse. When he reached Finown there was no one waiting for him on the banks of the river. So, having made his way, with some difficulty, over the stepping stones at the ford, he began running in the hope of catching up with him before he reached Blackwater Bridge where the broad river rushes through the glen and the scenery is wild and lonely and the neighbourhood had, from time out of mind, been deemed a favourite haunt of the "good" folk.

As he approached the bridge, the silvery moon was just rising and Daniel stopped to see if it was possible to hear the friendly tramp of the horse's hooves, but he heard nothing save the distant voice of the watchdog. He could see nothing apart from the shadows cast by the fir trees upon the stream beneath and the pale moonbeams that danced like fish upon the water. Although the Dunhallow piper was merry with drink and Nancy Walsh's company, the hairs at the back of his neck began to rise as he realised he was close to the eerie realm of Fairie. Knowing the power of music on these occasions, he decided to play his pipes in the hope that their music would guard him against any evil thing that may hover around his path. For some strange reason, the only tune he could wring out of his chanter was O'Carolan's "Receipt for Drinking Whiskey". He continued on his way, feeling a little braver, and then he thought he heard the sound of horse's hooves on

Above: The scenery was wild and lonely and the neighbourhood had, from time out of mind, been deemed a favourite haunt of the "good" folk.

the road and so he ceased his piping. Soon what Daniel thought was one horse became a hundred and in the distance he could just see dim figures of horsemen approaching. He jumped into the shelter of a nearby bush and on looking out as the horsemen passed he was surprised to see that on some of the horses he could distinguish the figures of persons that he knew to be long dead. What alarmed him most was seeing his friend Tom Tierney who he had spoken to that very evening in the public house and the horse that Tom rode that had been drowned in a bog hole a fortnight earlier. From these circumstances, Daniel surmised that the horsemen could be the Slua Sidhe, the Fairy Host. But because Tom was known to him, Daniel could not help himself calling out and asking him to help him on his way by giving him a ride.

Tom spurred his horse over to Daniel and lifted him onto it with a smile on his face. At that point Daniel heard the whole troupe laughing and then he experienced more fear than he had ever known in his whole life. His fear was further increased when he found that neither the horse nor the rider had the solidity of frame that he would normally feel. They seemed to form an indefinable something between shadow and substance. When at last they came to the crossroads that led to the Squire's house, the horsemen took the route that led away and when the piper attempted to alight or speak to his friend Tom, he found both his limbs and tongue equally incapable of movement. The troupe halted at the Fort of Doom near the River Araglin, and there he perceived a beautiful and stately palace, full of lights which even put to shame the lustre of the stars and the clear full moon. At this point Daniel was able to jump off the horse and he followed the company he was with into a great hall, in which was a full orchestra, playing strange instruments which Daniel had never seen before, and bards and druids in long white robes. An elderly man bearing a long white wand and with a long white beard almost touching the ground announced to the company "Daniel O'Leary, the Dun Hallow Piper".

The audience rose and cheered and clapped until the fairy castle shook with the sound. When the applause had dwindled, a beautiful lady stepped forward and picked up a stringed instrument and sang the following strain addressed to the astounded piper:

"Thy welcome O'Leary be joyous and high,
as this dwelling fairy can echo reply,
the clarseach and crotal and loud bara-boo,
shall sound not a note 'til we've music from you.

The bara-boo's wildness is meet for the fray,
the crotal's soft mildness for festival gay,
the clarseach is meeter for bower and hall,
but thy chanter sounds sweeter, far sweeter than all.

When thy fingers are flying the chanter along,
and the keys are replying in wildness of song,
the bagpipes are speaking such magical strain
as minstrels are seeking to rival in vain.

Shall bards of this dwelling admire each sweet tune,
as thy war-notes are swelling that erst were their own,
shall beauties of brightness and chieftains of might,
to thy brisk lay of lightness dance lightly tonight.

O'er harper and poet will place thy high seat,
O'Leary we owe it to piper so sweet,
and fairies are braiding (such favourite art thou),
fresh laurel unfading to circle thy brow.

Thy welcome O'Leary be joyous and high,
as the dwelling of fairy can echo reply,
the clarseach and crotal and loud bara-boo,
shall sound not a note 'til we've music from you."

Then a seat that glittered with jewels like a throne was brought forward for the amazed Daniel by a band of beautiful fairy damsels who placed a garland of shining laurel upon his head. The fairy ladies proffered a goblet of red wine to the entranced piper, inviting him to drink and then he began to play. Every tune brought fresh applause and frenzied dancing, and all declared that their hearts had never felt lighter and their feet had never beat truer. At length, intoxicated with both the applause and the wine, the piper sank into a deep sleep.

When he awoke he found himself at the same bush by the same river whence he had espied the Fairy Host in the first place but he was still holding his pipes. At first he thought that he had dreamed of fairies due to his over-indulgence in the punch that he had drunk with the fair Nancy Walsh and then he found that his brows were encircled by a wreath of laurel that Daniel O'Leary still keeps in his parlour today and it miraculously remains as fresh as the night he was given it.

79

Irish Music in Exile

England

Between 1845 and 1855 nearly 300,000 Irish moved to mainland Britain. Here they experienced many of the social problems which were confronting their relations in America. Lack of training in industry, language problems, poor health and poverty kept most of the Irish on the fringes of British society. Their families were crammed into dilapidated tenements, particularly in Liverpool, Manchester and London, which became Irish ghettos. Being Irish and Catholic in a hostile environment, they were forced to create self-sustaining communities with a network of social clubs and religious and political societies. By the end of the 19th century the newly established Gaelic League found many willing converts among the Irish in Britain.

London became a haven for Irish writers, singers, musicians and dancing masters. The Irish Folksong Society was founded in England's capital in 1903 and counted among its founders Alfred Percival Graves, father of the poet and novelist Robert Graves who wrote the extravagant but beautifully poetic fantasy "The White Goddess". These London-Irish literati and middle-class nationalists began to legitimise Irish dances in an attempt to avoid confusion with Scottish *ceilidhe*. The Kerry dancing master Patrick Reidy, who taught Irish dancing at the Bijou Theatre, set out to create a canon of authentic Irish dances. In evaluating authentic sources, he weeded out foreign elements such as quadrilles and schottisches. Even the dancing style of Connemara, which was more flat-footed than its Munster counterpart, was discouraged. The Munster style became the prime model for the emerging canon of national dances which still endures to this day.

Alongside this céilí dancing the céilí band in its present form began to emerge as a product of the London/Irish dance scene. The first band to call themselves a céilí band was the Tara Céilí Band which was set up to play for a St Patrick's Day dance in Notting Hill in 1918.

Canada

The cheapest crossing for Irish emigrants was to Quebec in Canada but on arrival there many of them found conditions little better than those they had left behind in Ireland. Widespread diseases and destitution soon became intractable problems for the authorities in Quebec. Quarantine stations were quickly established to deal with the crisis, the worst being Grosse Ile on the St Lawrence river where thousands of famine victims were buried in mass graves within sight of their new homeland. The Irish had actually become established in Quebec well before this influx of famine victims. Irish

soldiers who had left under the penal laws against the Catholics and had fought for the French had been given land grants during the 18th century and by 1851 Quebec City had an Irish population of over 9,000.

Group dances such as the quadrille and the Lancers had already been established there and were joined by solo dances like the "Quebecoise gigue" which was a fusion of Irish traditional step dancing and English clog dancing. In the gigue the dancer is expected to keep the upper body rigid and straight and step with the feet in the same way as Sean Nós dancing (as seen in *Riverdance*).

81

Above: Quebec, Canada 1860.

America

The largest influx of famine immigrants in the New World settled in the East Coast cities of America, from Boston to Baltimore. Most of them exchanged their rural backgrounds for alien urban settings and suffered racial discrimination from the white Anglo-Saxon Protestant settlers. Despite this, the immigrant Irish poured into the sprawling ghettos of industrial America and by 1850 26 per cent of the population of New York and 25 per cent of Chicago were Irish-born. By 1855 there were over 1.5 million Irish people living in the United States. Most of these immigrants arrived with Gaelic as their first language, but most of the songs that survive to this day in America are sung in English. The lyrics describe their mostly unpleasant experiences and a homeland without joy. The Irish role in the formation of American labour unions is documented in songs, particularly the clandestine work of the Molly Maguires who represented the struggling miners of Pennsylvania in the 1860s and 1870s.

Songs like "Drill Ye Tarriers, Drill" and "We're Bound for San Diego" are about migrant Irish workers on the canals and railroads. "Green Grow the Laurel" recalls the Mexican-American War of 1845–1847 in which many Irish soldiers lost their lives. The song "Paddy's Lamentation" documents the false promises that many Irish soldiers were given during the Civil War when they fought on the Union side. Over 150,000 lost their lives and many lost limbs.

Following the American Civil War, the western frontier began to attract many Irish settlers. Industries started to boom and urban life required entertainers, making Irish musicians real assets, particularly in the music hall industry. There was much cross-cultural fertilisation between the immigrants and the newly freed Afro-American slaves. The variety theatre was a mixture of music, comedy and novelty acts, providing employment and entertainment for thousands of Irish musicians and immigrants. It was here that the stage Irishman, the archetypal "Paddy", began to evolve.

However, by the 1870s the loose morals of the concert saloon gave way to a more refined form of entertainment which took place in alcohol-free establishments. This was called vaudeville and it dominated the course of Irish music in urban America over the next 50 years. In vaudeville Irish songs and dance tunes were mixed into the melting pot of American showbusiness and re-emerged, changed into a variety of commercial forms.

One of the most celebrated entertainers of the time was George M Cohan, the son of Irish famine immigrants, who became know as Mr Yankee Doodle Dandy. His songs such as "Give My Regards to Broadway" and "You're a Grand Old Flag" became great American anthems. James Cagney, another Irish-American, went on to play Cohan in the Academy Award-winning film entitled *Yankee Doodle Dandy* which was released in 1942 and told the story of several generations of the Cohan family.

As the Irish moved up the social ladder in urban America, so too did the musicians and their audiences. With the development of concert pitch uillean pipes, being either D or E flat, perfected in Philadelphia by the Taylor brothers in the late 19th century, the pipes were deemed more suitable for large concert hall audiences. A string of pipers' clubs also opened across the USA and, as the Irish immigrants became more respectable, opera stars, such as John McCormack, were invited to perform. Thomas Edison's recording machine had been improved by the start of the 20th century and Victrola and Columbia Records began issuing cylindrical recordings on a commercial basis. The first known Irish musicians to record on a cylinder were New York piper Billy Hannafin and virtuoso piper Patsy Touhey in 1898 and 1900 respectively.

Although most Irish immigrants preferred to settle in the cities of North America, others formed rural communities and many travelled west to Texas, taking their music with them. The first Irish settlers in the west were trappers and goldrush pioneers, when gold was discovered in California in 1849. By the end of the 19th century, Irish traditional music was extremely popular in San Francisco which had its own pipers' club. Unfortunately, the 1906 earthquake put an end to this.

Irish musicians also shared their music with the indigenous people of America. Cross-fertilisation of the two cultures reached its peak in the Athabaskan communities of Alaska. It was not only the music but the dancing that blended and Athabaskan dancers still favour close-to-the-floor stepping styles. Bill Stevens, the Athabaskan fiddler, has guested with the Chieftains.

*Above: Most of the songs that survive to this day
in America are sung in English. The lyrics describe
their mostly unpleasant experiences and a
homeland without joy.*

Biography: Francis O'Neill

Francis O'Neill was born in Tralibane, County Cork, in the year of the Potato Famine on 28 August 1848. He was the youngest of seven children and he spent his youth in this Irish-speaking rural area, surrounded by musicians. Like many other Irish boys at that time, he was pulled by the spirit of adventure to move away from his homeland and at the age of 16 signed on as a cabin boy on an English merchant vessel. During the following years he sailed to Russia, Egypt, the West Indies, Mexico, South America, Hawaii, Japan and the United States.

On one of his travels he met Anna Rogers, an Irish girl, and they married. He and Anna arrived in Chicago in 1871, just after the Great Fire, in order to start a family. After various labouring jobs he joined the Chicago police force in August 1873 and very quickly rose through the ranks.

The Irish first began to settle in Chicago in the 1830s where they were employed in large numbers to dig the Illinois and Michigan Canal. Most of these early settlers were from County Cork and many had already gained experience building the Erie Canal in Pennsylvania. They congregated near the south branch of the Chicago river, where neighbourhoods like Canaryville, Brighton Park and Connelly's Patch became known as Irish strongholds. By the time Francis O'Neill arrived, the Irish formed around 30 per cent of the population of Chicago, some 40,000 people. Many of them played traditional Irish music. By the turn of the century that figure had risen to more than 235,000.

Francis O'Neill became Chief Superintendent of Police in 1901 and supervised over 3,000 officers, two-thirds of whom were Irish. He reputedly would roam the streets looking for Irish musicians to recruit into his police force. O'Neill had an abiding love of traditional Irish music that he had absorbed during his childhood. In the 1880s he met James O'Neill (no relation), a fiddler, and another police recruit who was to become sergeant, from County Down who had a huge store of dance tunes plus the added bonus of being able to write music. The two O'Neills formed a lifelong friendship, both as police officers and as aficionados of Irish music. Both would spend their spare time around the dance halls, saloons and vaudeville theatres, as well as the streets searching out musicians and writing out their tunes. Even on the streetcars Francis would stop and listen to hummed-out melodies which he would then repeat back to Sergeant O'Neill who would write them down. In 1903 he published his first book, *The Music of Ireland*, which contained the largest collection of dance tunes ever published with 1,850 melodies including 625 song airs, 415 double jigs, 380 reels, 225

hornpipes, 75 Carolan harp tunes, 60 slip jigs, 50 marches and 20 long dances – in all, over two decades of work.

He wrote most of his works after he resigned for political reasons in 1905. He began to travel and collect music even more avidly. In 1906 he and his wife spent six weeks in Ireland where he collected a huge repertoire of dance tunes from players like Paddy MacNamara in East Clare (his wife's birthplace). On his return to Chicago he published a second collection of tunes called *The Dance Music of Ireland* containing 1,001 tunes, followed immediately by *Waifs and Strays of Gaelic Melody* and a book called *Irish Music* which featured piano accompaniments. He also began work on his book *Irish Folk Music: A Fascinating*

Hobby, which he published in 1910. The book contained an unprecedented amount of information about Irish music history. He continued the ethno-biographical process in his book *Irish Minstrels and Musicians* which included a large collection of essays on pipers and harpers. It also contained a collection of contemporary photographs, music transcripts and traditional Irish folktales.

O'Neill died at home from heart failure in 1936 and was buried in the family mausoleum in Mount Olivet cemetery in Mount Greenwood, Chicago.

It is certain that without Captain O'Neill's dedication to collecting Irish folk music it would most likely have been lost for all time.

Above: Francis O'Neill.

Cruiscín Lán (Traditional)

Let the farmer praise his grounds, let the
huntsman praise his hounds,
Let the shepherd praise his dewy-scented
lawn.
Oh but I'm more wise than they, spend
each happy night and day
With my darlin' little cruiscín lán, lán, lán,
My darlin' little cruiscín lán.

Oh, gradh mo chroide mo cruiscín Slainte
geal Mauverneen
(Oh, graw moh kree moh krooshkeen
Slawnta gal Mohvoorneen)
Gradh mo chroide mo cruiscín lán, lán, lán
(Graw moh kree moh krooshkeen lawn,
lawn, lawn)
Oh, gradh mo chroide mo cruiscín lán
(Oh, graw moh kree moh krooshkeen
lawn)

Immortal and divine, Great Bacchus, god
of wine,
Create me by adoption your own son
In hopes that you'll comply that my glass
shall ne'er run dry
Nor my darlin' little cruiscín lán, lán, lán,
My darlin' little cruiscín lán.

Oh, gradh mo chroide mo cruiscín Slainte
geal Mauverneen
Gradh mo chroide mo cruiscín lán, lán, lán
Oh, gradh mo chroide mo cruiscín lán.

Oh, when cruel death appears in a few but
happy years
You'll say: "Oh, won't you come along
with me?"
I'll say: "Begone, you knave, for King
Bacchus gave me lave
To take another cruiscín lán, lán, lán
To take another cruiscín lán."

Oh, gradh mo chroide mo cruiscín Slainte
geal Mauverneen
Gradh mo chroide mo cruiscín lán, lán, lán
Oh, gradh mo chroide mo cruiscín lán.

Then fill your glasses high, let's not part
with lips so dry
For the lark now proclaims it is the dawn
And since we can't remain, may we shortly
meet again
To fill another cruiscín lán, lán, lán,
To fill another cruiscín lán.

Oh, gradh mo chroide mo cruiscín Slainte
geal Mauverneen
Gradh mo chroide mo cruiscín lán, lán, lán
Oh, gradh mo chroide mo cruiscín lán.

Story: Donagh an Asal

Many long years ago, in an obscure Galway village, there was a piper nicknamed Donagh an Asal, on account of the donkey which served him as a beast of burden in various capacities. Naturally, he was poor, like all of his tribe, but that did not deter a pretty young colleen from taking a liking to him, in preference to many eligible young men of the parish, presumably on account of his musical talent.

We all know what to expect from early marriages, so we can understand that the poor piper had no easy time of it, providing for an ever-increasing family, particularly as he had no other means of supporting them than by his humble profession as a piper. Much as the local peasantry admired and enjoyed his music, their own poverty kept a check on their generosity. So it was with Donagh's family as it was with many others. The eldest child kept leaving one by one as the newest arrived and the time came when even the last one, a boy, made up his mind to leave home like his brothers and sisters before him and seek employment amongst strangers. With all her children who she nursed and tended with a mother's self-sacrificing care gone from her, it is little wonder that anxiety and grief soon undermined the health of Donagh's wife who did not long survive the departure of the last of her children. The poor piper's condition was now pitiable indeed, with his faithful and beloved wife dead in the house and not a single child of theirs in the country to attend the wake or funeral of their mother. All Donagh possessed in the

world besides his pipes and a few bits of furniture was the donkey and cart used mostly to haul home a crate of turf from the bog to keep his poor fire going. The poor sad beast, it must be admitted, was almost as tired of the world as his owner. The attendance at the wake was very disappointing to the bereaved piper, although, like all his race, he had made every possible arrangement to give her a decent burial. Barely, enough men to convey the coffin to the donkey cart came to the house on the morning of the funeral. The expense of having a hearse could not be entertained at all, but this he did not mind, if only the attendance came up to his expectations, for indeed a kind mother and a good neighbour deserved that much respect anyway.

As the funeral was just about ready to move, a most unexpected thing happened. Prompted by his grief and humiliation Donagh an Asal ran into the house for his pipes, mounted the cart, took his seat on the coffin and, buckling on his instrument, struck up a lament. The wailing of the pipes, besides affording the grief-stricken widower a means of giving vent to his feelings, attracted everyone to it within hearing range and by the time they had reached the graveyard, which was over three miles from the house, the funeral turned out to be the largest which ever entered the gates of the graveyard in that part of the country, such is the power of the music of the pipes.

Irish Music in the Twentieth Century

Irish Independence

In 1916, Sinn Fein's armed rebellion began. In 1917 they defeated the Irish Parliamentary Party at the by-elections and replaced them almost completely in the general election of 1918. The following year they formed the Dáil Eireann, the Irish Assembly, and refused to take their seats at Westminster. The British forces in their attempt to crush Sinn Fein sparked off a guerrilla warfare campaign, led by Michael Collins of the IRA. Lloyd George, the British prime minister, brought in the Government of Ireland Act which became law in December 1920. The following year the Anglo-Irish Treaty was signed in which 26 counties gained independence as the Irish Free State but still remained within the British Commonwealth. Six of Ulster's counties had already been granted their own assembly and still remain part of the United Kingdom. However, the establishment of the free state provoked a bitter civil war between government forces and the men of the IRA who opposed the treaty. In May 1923 a truce was negotiated but this civil war left a legacy of hatred, revenge and clan and family feuds which sadly continue to this day.

Above: Michael Collins.

90

Irish Radio

The middle classes who had vested interests in the economic stability of Ireland governed with social and cultural conservatism. In 1923 the Censorship of Films Act was passed and in 1929 the Censorship of Publications Act followed. These edicts were orchestrated by the Irish Vigilance Societies and the Catholic Truth Society of Ireland, who next turned their attention towards Irish traditional music.

In rural Ireland the Catholic clergy were concerned about women's fashions, immodest dress, indecent and unsupervised, dancing, theatrical performances, cinema exhibitions, evil literature, drinks, strikes and lockouts, motor cars, jazz and unlicensed dance halls. The priests were particularly concerned that they were unable to supervise the activities of the youngsters in rural communities because the motor car and the bus had allowed the movement of young people to anywhere they pleased – with the result that a dance at a pub in a quiet country parish could be attended by youth from a long way away. The clergy expended a great deal of effort in trying to curb what they saw as acts of unbridled immorality happening in their parishes. The state, in its efforts to bring about a national identity, began broadcasting football and hurling matches on the radio.

By 1926 the campaign to rid the countryside of foreign and therefore sinful music was underway with a vengeance. In order to find a solution to safeguard the morality of his parishioners Father Tom Larkin created the Ballinakil Traditional Players, to play for céilí dances in the Ballinakil and Woodford parts of East Galway. The band, which was made up of members of the rural farming community, comprised mostly flautists and fiddlers. Father Larkin coached the players and got them to rehearse common versions of tunes. He also transcribed their own repertoire so a piano player could read the melody line and arrange their own bass chords. Father Larkin's experiment brought together musicians from both ends of the social spectrum. In 1928 the band played at the Athlone Feis (festival). They made numerous live broadcasts from 2RN and recorded with Parlophone in the 1930s. These pioneer recordings were the benchmarks against which other céilí bands rated themselves.

Radios were a luxury in rural Ireland and few people owned them; even fewer owned the wind-up gramophones. Their presence became more common during the 1930s and many were sent to their families from

America where they were considerably cheaper. These new-fangled machines met with a mixed reaction among the rural communities. Some musicians welcomed an opportunity to hear new tunes whereas others felt threatened by the virtuosity of the performances that they heard on the recordings. Unfortunately both of these reactions led to a decline in regional styles of playing. For set dancers the gramophone opened up more possibilities by allowing them to practise their dances without a band. The quality of the gramophone music was usually superior to that of local dance bands but the records stopped playing before the dance ended so the dancers would have to stop in order to wind up the gramophone again, before completing their figure.

In 1936 EMI Records set up a recording studio in Dublin, designed to develop native talent and promote record buying in Ireland. One of the most prolific musicians recording during this time was the piper Leo Rowsome who taught piping at the Dublin College of Music from 1922 until the day he died in 1970.

The Emigrants Return

By 1932 Eamonn de Valera formed the Fianna Fáil party which won 72 out of the 153 seats in the Irish Assembly. With the help of the Labour Party de Valera set up a government which went on to dominate Irish politics for almost four decades. He immediately abolished the oath of allegiance to the English monarchy and withheld loan repayments by Irish farmers to their former British landlords. Britain retaliated by imposing heavy import duties and this economic war continued until 1938 when the Irish government agreed to pay the British government a sum of £10 million in order to settle the debts. This was a time of extreme hardship in rural Ireland. Almost 30,000 people left because of the austere conditions that were being imposed upon them. The early years of de Valera's government had an atmosphere of repressive Puritanism about them and the Public Dance Halls Act was passed in 1935 in order to control public morality by banning country house dances. Many musicians and set dancers left the country. However, it was also a time when the parish priests built new village halls where the céilí bands flourished. It was not Irish music that the government was trying to stamp out but the foreign imports of jazz and, later on, blues and rock 'n' roll, which they believed to be corrupting influences on the nation's youth. Despite these upheavals some pockets of traditional music survived, particularly in Sligo, Leitrim, Galway, Clare and Kerry.

The Folklore Commission which was set up in 1935 sent its collectors to these rural areas in a bid to save the country's treasures of music and song from oblivion.

When World War II broke out in 1939 the Irish Free State decided to remain neutral. The war years were times of fastidious censorship and rationing but despite the paranoia Ireland was never of sufficient importance, for once, for either side to invade. With the ending of the war the Irish were ready for a change of government and Fianna Fáil lost the election. A new inter-party coalition government was founded and was led by John A Costello. By the end of 1948 the Republic of Ireland Act was passed, which withdrew Ireland officially from the British Commonwealth. Despite a new government taking power, emigration from rural Ireland continued to empty the country. Many left for Britain and found work in the Midlands. Irish "Navvies" and construction workers found employment rebuilding London after the Blitz. London became particularly popular with Irish musicians and three nights a week the Tara Club on Brixton Road played an eclectic mix of Irish and modern dances. Many musicians from the rural areas also began flocking to Dublin and the Dublin Pipers' Club in Thomas Street became a meeting place for traditional musicians from all over the country.

Since 1947 the BBC had been making a valuable collection of traditional Irish music by recording rural as well as urban-based performers. In 1951 Séamus Ennis joined the BBC and over the next seven years built up a huge library of recordings from all over the British Isles and Ireland. These archives of over 1,500 performances, which were also broadcast, are an astounding achievement in the documentation of traditional Irish music. Traditional Irish music programmes also began to become very popular on Radio Eireann and, with the assistance of mobile recording units, many sessions were taped in rural locations.

The Fleadh Cheoil Movement

In January 1951 members of the Dublin Pipers' Club decided to organise a *fleadh cheoil* (music festival) at the Whit weekend in Mullingar, County Westmeath. Invitations were issued to musicians from all over Ireland and the festival proved to be a great success. In September that year Comhaltas Ceoltoiri Eireann held their inaugural meeting to ensure it would become a regular national festival and, by 1956, the festival had indeed become a national event and featured pageants, parades and music competitions. It attracted legendary performers such as Paddy Canny, Paddy Carthy, Paddy Murphy, Elizabeth Crotty and Willy Clancy. The climax of the *fleadh* was the All Ireland Céilí Band Competition. It is still the premier event in Ireland's musical calendar and now brings together traditional Irish musicians from all over the world as well as the audiences who come to see them perform.

Molly Malone

In Dublin's fair city, where the girls are so pretty,
I first set my eyes on sweet Molly Malone
As she wheeled her wheelbarrow through streets broad and narrow,
Crying cockles and mussels alive a-live O!

A-live a-live O! A-live a-live O!
Crying cockles and mussels alive a-live O!

She was a fishmonger and sure it was no wonder
For so were her father and mother before
And they both wheeled their barrows through streets broad and narrow,
Crying cockles and mussels alive a-live O!

A-live a-live O! A-live a-live O!
Crying cockles and mussels alive a-live O!

She died of a fever and no one could save her
And that was the end of sweet Molly Malone
Now her ghost wheels her barrow through streets broad and narrow,
Crying cockles and mussels alive a-live O!

A-live a-live O! A-live a-live O!
Crying cockles and mussels alive a-live O!
A-live a-live O! A-live a-live O!
Crying cockles and mussels alive a-live O!

One of the most important Irish composers was Sean Ó Riada. He not only kept traditional music alive but helped it evolve in new directions.

Biography: Sean Ó Riada

Sean Ó Riada was born in 1931 in Cork. During his youth, after having moved to Limerick, he learned to play the fiddle. He attended University College in Cork and graduated with a music degree in 1952. He was then appointed Assistant Music Director at Radio Eireann between 1954 and 1955. At the end of 1953 he had travelled to mainland Europe in order to study music there and was particularly influenced by the compositions of Schoenberg. On returning to Ireland in 1955 he was appointed Musical Director of the Abbey Theatre in Dublin where he stayed for seven years.

Ó Riada wrote a number of compositions using Irish traditional music but with a modern edge. These include works such as the Greek-titled *Nomos 1–6*, his 1956 pastoral piece *The Banks of Sullane*, and *The Lords and the Bards* in 1959. He also wrote scores for *Saoirse*, for the documentary *Mise Eire*, and for *The Playboy of the Western World* which featured the music of Ceoltóirí Chualann, a group that he had put together in the late 1950s consisting of fiddlers John Kelly, Sean Keane and the founding members of the Chieftains. Ó Riada carefully crafted a new and dynamic inter-rural traditional folk music, bringing it away from pub sessions into the concert halls of the world. He revived compositions of the harper Turlough O'Carolan which until then had been almost forgotten.

Apart from being a composer and a musician, he also broadcast a series called *Our Musical Heritage* on Radio Eireann which introduced a new audience to traditional folk music. His influence on the formalising of traditional musical forms in the modern world cannot be overemphasised.

From 1963 until his death in 1971 he also lectured in music at University College Cork.

95

Above: Sean Ó Riada.

Biography: The Chieftains

The original founding members met in the late 1950s as part of the Sean Ó Riada folk orchestra which was trying to create an authentic Irish sound at a time when interest had seriously diminished in the form. In 1962 they started out as the Chieftains. The members were Paddy Moloney (uillean pipes and tin whistle), Sean Potts (tin whistle), Michael Tubridy (flute, concertina and tin whistle) and Martin Fay (fiddle). The band released its first album in 1963 and they remained semi-professional until their album *Chieftains 4*. Their next album, *Chieftains 5*, was their debut with Island Records and saw the likes of Eric Clapton, Mick Jagger and Emmylou Harris all guesting. The Chieftains also featured on a Mike Oldfield album and a Stanley Kubrick soundtrack. All this led to their reaching a wider audience.

Above: The Chieftains.

96

In 1976 Matt Molloy, a former member of the Bothy Band and Planxty, joined the line-up as arranger and flautist. The band has seen many changes in personnel over the years, although Paddy Moloney and Martin Fay still remain from the original line-up.

During the 1980s they again collaborated on soundtracks and also worked with artists such as Van Morrison and James Galway.

The 1990s saw them work alongside many star line-ups including Marianne Faithfull, the Corrs, Joni Mitchell, Los Lobos and Ry Cooder. However, in 2000 they released their album *Water From The Well* which saw them concentrating on their own style of music again. They also celebrated their 40th anniversary in 2002 with their *The Wide World Over* album. Since their inception they have released over 40 other albums.

97

Above: Van Morrison with Paddy Moloney of the Chieftains.

Story: Fairy Tunes

Padraig O'Halloran was a jocular old wood ranger who lived on a small farm, rent-free, in consideration of his services as an estate bailiff for the local gentry. The farm was situated on the brow of a hill, overlooking a lonely valley. One fine, calm night, about 11 o'clock, just as he was beginning to get ready for bed, he heard the mellow tones of a flute wafting on the summer air, through the open window. At first he thought his sense of hearing was faulty, but on moving closer to the window to listen, all doubt disappeared, for sure enough there was music coming from the glen.

What struck him most was that the tune, a fine, lively Irish jig, played in dancing time, was unknown to him and he had memorised a huge stock of popular tunes himself, to which he used to jig about and play upon a jews harp he always carried. He was quite certain that he had not heard this tune anywhere before. He listened in rapt attention, intent on memorising it and then he got to wondering who could be playing a flute so late at night, in a lonesome glen, far away from any human habitation except his own humble cottage.

He got to wondering whether it was the fairies themselves holding revels and dancing on the green. After all, his cottage overlooked three fairie mounds and a giant's grave, just across the river and opposite his own front door. Padraig, determined to solve the mystery, stepped out into the open fields and proceeded quietly in the direction of the mysterious music.

Just like trying to follow the end of a rainbow, the music eluded him. It was everywhere and nowhere and, brave as he was, his nerves failed him. He suddenly decided there was no place like home after all. No sooner had he determined on retracing his steps and before he had time to turn around, than the invisible musician, to his consternation, had taken up position right behind him. As the perplexed Padraig advanced on his way home, the fairy fluter preceded him with an unflagging persistence. Suddenly the first clarion crow of the cock on the roost sounded, heralding the turn of the night, and the music ceased with startling abruptness and poor Padraig entered his home, almost in a state of collapse.

To his dying day the wood ranger vouched for the truth of the story in all its mystifying details and in corroboration of his claims pointed to the fact that neither he nor any of the other local musicians knew the tune or had ever heard it before, so where else could it come from if not from the fairies?

Irish Music Today

The Swinging Sixties

The Swinging Sixties were as important musically in Ireland as they were throughout the rest of the western world. Ireland became less insular, native industry was boosted with foreign investment and economic prosperity returned along with many emigrants. New schools and housing estates were built and a general feeling of affluence prevailed for the first time. The lounge bar replaced the public house and modern consumerism replaced the austerity and conservatism of the previous era. The television phenomenon was beamed into bars and homes throughout the country and bus loads of wealthy tourists and foreign motor cars became the norm. Adding to these changes was the liberalism of the second Vatican Council which alleviated the authoritarianism so prevalent in Irish Catholicism. Musicians, like all other parts of the community, thrived under these conditions. Their predecessors had played in kitchens and village halls, but traditional Irish music had now became so popular that it had moved into larger venues such as the clubs which now opened their doors for the first time to women. Musicians now became paid employees and a dynamic relationship blossomed between the proprietors of entertainment establishments and the entertainers.

As the musicians left their rural céilí band audiences, they began to form trios and quartets. Their repertoires changed as their new patrons had more eclectic tastes. They began to learn Top 20 ballads and to mix jigs and reels with jives and twists. American music brought over by tourists seeking their heritage also influenced the local musicians greatly. These tourists also demanded to hear what they believed to be authentic traditional Irish music.

In America itself the folk revival taking place through artists such as Bob Dylan and Joan Baez was joined by Tommy Makem and the Clancys who sang their ballads with an enthusiastic delivery rarely heard on the more conservative American stage of the early 1960s. They performed at Carnegie Hall in New York and then left for the UK to sing at the Royal Albert Hall.

In Ireland, as elsewhere, the recording industry also prospered. During the late 1950s Gael Linn produced a seminal series of recordings on 78 rpm records by fiddlers such as Sean Ryan, Dennis Murphy and both the aforementioned Paddy Canny and the piper Willy Clancy, all of whom were masters of their craft. The first LP record of Irish traditional music was recorded in 1960 entitled *All Ireland Champions* and featured fiddlers Paddy Canny and P J Hayes alongside Peadar O'Loughlin and pianist Bridey Lafferty. Throughout the 1960s the ballad boom introduced a generation of guitar groups into the pubs of the nation. The most well-known of these are the

The Dubliners

The Dubliners were formed in 1962, and played in Donoghue's Bar in Dublin, under the name of the Ronnie Drew Group. The original members were Ronnie Drew, Barney MacKenna, Luke Kelly and Ciarán Bourke. They had all been singing and performing individually in the city's folk clubs before they joined together.

In 1964 Kelly left the group and went to England. Two other members then joined, these being Bob Lynch and John Sheehan. The band continued to play the pub and theatre circuit and made several albums on the Transatlantic label which gained them a strong following on the Irish folk scene. Dominic Behan introduced them to Phil Solomon who became their manager and they began recording on his own label, Major Minor. In 1965 they became full-time professional musicians and Kelly returned to play with them replacing Lynch. Throughout their career each member has pursued his own project, including Luke Kelly's stints as actor.

In 1966, the Dubliners were played constantly on Radio Caroline, the hip pirate station, and a year later they made an appearance on Top of the Pops playing a censored version of the bawdy "Seven Drunken Nights", followed up by the song "Black Velvet Band". They continued to produce other hits, both singles and albums and were soon to become an international concert attraction.

Dubliners, the Wolf Tones, the Fureys and the Johnstones. There were also a number of new céilí bands at this time, particularly the Castle Céilí Band who became national heroes after their appearance at the Fleadh Cheoil. A blend of youth and experience, the band were resident at O'Donaghue's in Merrion Row, Dublin, one of the few places in Dublin where traditional musicians could escape the onslaught of the pop ballad boom and which is still one of Dublin's most popular pubs.

The number of artists that cite the Dubliners as one of their major influences and idols is tremendous. The Dubliners have brought Irish folk music to millions all over the world in a way that no emigration ever has.

101

Above: Tommy Makem.

Above: The Dubliners. In 1966, the Dubliners were played constantly on Radio Caroline, the hip pirate station.

Ciarán Bourke retired in 1974 and when Kelly became ill in the 1980s Sean Cannon joined the band. Kelly passed away in 1984.

In 1987 they played with the Pogues on the hit single "The Irish Rover" which was to open up a completely new audience for them. Eamonn Campbell joined them on a regular basis. In 1988 Ciarán Bourke died. They celebrated their 30th anniversary in 1992 with a double-CD and an extensive tour and in 1995 Ronnie Drew left and Paddy Reilly took his place.

In 2002 the Dubliners released their 40th anniversary album and they continue to tour to this day amid rumours that they are about to break up.

During the 1970s, after Ireland's entry into the EC, there was a high level of regional development, improved educational standards and new levels of Irish tourism. The youth of the nation was now deeply affected by mainstream American pop culture. Traditional musicians were also being swept along by the economic and social changes which were altering the course of Irish life. It soon became apparent that Irish traditional music had moved beyond its old local, rural setting and entered the realm of popular culture. Schools too began making traditional music part of their curriculum for the first time.

Above: The Dubliners.

The Pogues

The band the Pogues formed as a blend of the listening habits of its founder members Shane MacGowan and James Fearnley, that is the London punk scene of the early 70s/80s and traditional Irish music. Originally called Pogue mo Thoin, which is Gaelic for "Kiss my ****", they changed their name to the Pogues after a number of complaints.

Many of the band members learnt to play traditional Irish instruments in an unconventional way, by effectively being told to pick up and play. For instance, Peter "Spider" Stacey, had originally started off in the band with no musical talent whatsoever but was allowed on stage to scream into the microphone. Rather than sacking him for his superfluous role, he was given a tin whistle and after practicing daily became the band's whistle player. Jem Finer swapped from his punk band guitar to the banjo and mandolin and when the band needed an accordion player, James Fearnley, a talented pianist, suddenly found himself having to learn the accordion. The group's anarchic stage show, often resulted in drunken brawls between band members yet this ensured that their audiences were kept entertained. After adding Andrew Ranken on drums and Cait O'Riordan on bass and being asked to open for The Clash, they released their first album, "Red Roses for Me" in 1984. Although a number of the songs were traditional on the album, it was McGowan's skillful song writing talents that captured his Ireland of the time in songs such as "Streams of Whiskey".

Since then the band has released a number of Top 20 albums and has undergone a number of line-up changes. Their political stance ensured controversy with their protest song "Birmingham Six" which was subsequently banned from the airwaves and the video to their single "A Pair of Brown Eyes" was censored, owing to band members spitting on a poster of then UK Prime Minister Margaret Thatcher. They teamed up with producer Steve Lillywhite who added a Middle Eastern aspect to their sound. At Christmas in 1987 they had a No 2 hit with the ironically humourous "Fairytale of New York" featuring a duet between MacGowan and the late singer Kirsty MacColl, the wife of Lillywhite.

In 1992 Shane MacGowan left the band, largely due to his alcoholism and a number of tour dates that he had been unable to fulfil, and was replaced first by Joe Strummer of the Clash (now sadly deceased) and then Spider Stacy took over in 1992. The Pogues continued until 1996 when they decided to go their own ways; MacGowan in the meantime had his own band The Popes.

In 2001 the Pogues briefly reformed for some live tour dates, again with MacGowan on vocals. MacGowan sadly has been unable to win his fight against alcohol but continues with the attitude of the band's original name.

Above: The Pogues.

The King of the Fairies

The King of the Fairies was probably the most well-known piece of Irish traditional music played by "Celtic" rock groups during the 1970s. This phenomenon witnessed the melding of Afro-American with Celtic and European folk music and instrumentation forming a hybrid. The group that stood out the most at this time was undoubtedly Planxty, featuring the uillean pipes of Liam Óg Ó Floinn as well as a Balkan bouzouki with singers Christy Moore, Donal Lunny and Andy Irvine.

De Danann, taking their name from the fairy tribe, formed in 1973 and mixed fiddles, accordions, bodhran and banjo with the bouzouki. In 1975 the Bothy Band arrived on the scene, bringing their rhythmically powerful and melodically fast music to both Irish and international audiences. Although they only released four albums before disbanding in 1979 their fiery music is unforgettable. Other groups vying for attention at this time included Stockton's Wing, Stocker's Lodge, Skylark, Buttons and Bows and the jazz-oriented band Moving Hearts which again featured Christy Moore.

The 1970s and 1980s were years of experimentation but during the 1990s there was a return to the regional source of Irish music, evident particularly in the melodic style and repertoire of the Donegal group Altan who combine authentic Sean Nós songs with polished instrumentals. Altan became one of the most successful Irish groups to perform on the international circuit.

During this time there was also a number of orchestral works released, mixing classical and traditional music. The piping of Liam Óg Ó Floinn and the music of composer Sean Davey joined together in *The Brendan Voyage*, *The Pilgrim*, *Granuaile* and *The Relief of the Siege of Derry*.

Above: Christy Moore – singer in a number of Irish supergroups.

In 1991 fiddler Charlie Lennon released his *Ireland Wedding*, a work in 16 movements for traditional instruments and orchestra.

A steady stream of exchange has also taken place between other Celtic nations and Ireland, particularly Brittany, through festivals held in Lorient Douarnenez and Paimpol which frequently invite Irish musicians to perform. Breton musicians are also invited to perform at Irish festivals; particularly well known is the harper Alan Stivell.

During the decade of the nineties Ireland became inundated by music lovers from all over the world heading to the Emerald Isle to hear authentic Irish music. The EC has created an enormous market for Irish musicians to reach and many European cities have developed their own Irish music communities.

Doolin

Doolin, a small fishing village in North Clare, first became a musical mecca in the 1970s with thousands of rucksacked hippies arriving from Europe and North America to visit. Since then this small village nestling between the cliffs of Moher, the Burren and the Aran Islands has hosted a non-stop session of music. Doolin consists of three pubs, a few hostels, bed and breakfasts and a number of castles including Doonagore and Doonmacfelim. Doolin was Gaeltacht well into the 1970s – that is, native Celtic.

It was the Russell brothers, Packie, Gussy and Miko (one of the last Sean Nós singers in Clare), who created the "Russell Memorial Weekend" which takes place on the last weekend of February every year and which causes people to flock to this amazing little village from all around the globe.

109

Above: The cliffs of Moher.

Willy Clancy's Summer School

Willy Clancy was born on Christmas Eve 1918 in County Clare. His mother Ellen played the concertina and his father Gilbert the flute and concertina. Gilbert Clancy had learned his music from the blind piper Garrett Barry. Although Garrett had died penniless in the local workhouse 19 years before young Willy was born his ghost was said to haunt the Clancy house. As a young man, Willy played the flute like his father and then he heard the travelling piper Johnny Doran playing the uillean pipes. In 1938 he acquired a bag and chanter from Doran's brother Felix.

Like his father, Willy was a carpenter and after serving his apprenticeship he moved first to Dublin and then to London. In 1947, he won first prize at the Oireachtas Piping Competition in Dublin. When his father died in 1957 Clancy returned to Miltown Malbay. That same year he recorded for Gael Linn two classic pieces of Irish piping on a rare Maloney chanter, made in Knockerra in 1860. Over the next 18 years, Willy held court in Friel's pub in his hometown and pipers, singers and storytellers from all walks of life came there to listen to him.

He died in January 1973 but a group of his friends decided to create a living monument to him. The Willy Clancy Summer School 80 students and a small faculty of teachers. Now it is an international forum for Irish traditional music; each year over a thousand students from all over the world and teachers from universities come there to take part in master classes and workshops for instrumental music (pipes, whistle, flute, concertina, accordion and fiddle), traditional singing and set dancing. The Summer School is the primary meeting place in the world for Na Píobairí Uillean, the Irish Pipers' Association, which Willy formed in 1968. The Willy Clancy Summer School has inspired many other schools across Ireland, which follow a similar format.

Side note: Na Píobairí Uillean – The Irish Pipers Association – teaches weekly classes in Dublin, as well as throughout Ireland. It organises weekend classes in pipe maintenance such as reed-making and ensures that the tradition is passed on to new musicians. They archive traditional pipe music and host exhibits all over the world. Indeed their international membership has now surpassed a thousand in number.

Above: Traditional Irish musical instruments and dancing, continues to delight and inspire people of all ages.

Riverdance

The *Riverdance* phenomenon has been instrumental in bringing Irish traditional music and dancing to the world stage. It began simply as a seven-minute interval piece for Ireland's entry in the 1994 Eurovision Song Contest. Over 300 million television viewers were thrilled with what they saw and as a bonus, Ireland won the Eurovision Song Contest that year and no one can ever forget what they witnessed on that magical night.

Because of huge public demand, the producers decided to release a video and a single and this only whetted the public's appetite even more and so Moya Docherty and her husband John McColgan and composer Bill Whelan decided to put together a full two-hour stage show. It was decided to give the show an international feeling, instead of making it purely Irish. They brought in musical and dance talents from all over the world, including Maria Pages, a Flamenco dancer from Spain, the Moiseyev Folk Ballet Company from Russia, a Gospel choir from Atlanta, Georgia, New York tap dancers and many others. The show made its premiere at the Point Depot Theatre in Dublin on 9 February 1995. It ran for five weeks and every performance was sold out. The show was also released on video and immediately became a best-seller. Owing to demand for the show being so huge, the management decided to take the show to London where they opened on 6

June 1995 at the specially refurbished Apollo Hammersmith. It then travelled to New York, bringing Irish dancing to the huge number of descendants of the Irish immigrants who had arrived there in the centuries before.

Irish Music Today

During the summer of 1996, while playing again at the Apollo London, it was decided to create two separate touring companies – the Liffey Company who were to tour Europe and Australia, New Zealand and Japan, and the Lee Company for touring in North America. In September 1997 *Riverdance* celebrated its thousandth show which was performed simultaneously in England and the USA. In

January 1998, a third company, called the Lagan Company, made their debut in Vancouver, Canada. Michael Flatley, one of the company's early stars, has since formed his own Irish step dancing extravaganza called *Lord of the Dance* which has also met with international acclaim.

Riverdance continues to evolve and amaze new audiences throughout the world.

113

Above: Scene from Riverdance.

Technology and the Internet

The internet has meant that a network of musicians and music lovers can discover and learn all about Irish music, even if they are never likely to set foot in Ireland.

Numerous resources exist from archives of traditional songs to musical instrument makers. There are many internet radio stations and discussion boards entirely dedicated to traditional Irish music.

Biography: Clannad

Clannad is the Gaelic word for family and indeed this is an appropriate name for the band as it consists of family members, the Brennans (Maire and her two brothers Pol and Cieran from a family of nine) and the Duggans (Padraig and Noel – both uncles to the Brennans). The Brennan family come from County Donegal. The Brennans' father Leo had been in a showband before he opened a tavern

Above: Clannad.

114

and their mother was a music teacher. They had also learned a great deal of the Gaelic myths and legends by listening to tales told by their maternal grandparents.

In 1970 Clannad started by playing in Leo Brennan's bar, at first doing covers of pop songs of the time which they would then play at local dances. However, it was not long before they started to tap into their heritage by playing Irish folk music. Soon the band members were asking local musicians to teach them traditional songs and Clannad started to acquire a collection of these, which went into the hundreds. However, they were constantly being told

that they would not get anywhere by singing Gaelic songs. Fortunately they continued to work at it because they loved the music so much. It was not long before they were touring colleges and they also managed to earn a recording contract after winning the Letterkenny Folk Festival.

In the 1970s Clannad went on to record six traditional albums, including tunes by Turlough O'Carolan. Their first album *Clannad* was released in 1973. They also toured Europe which culminated in them turning professional in 1976 after earning a standing ovation in Berlin.

Above: Clannad.

In 1980 Enya Brennan, one of the sisters of the Brennans, joined the band for two albums *Crann Ull* and *Fuaim*. She sang and played keyboards but left in 1982 to pursue her solo career, and has proved to be an extremely successful artist in her own right.

The band continued to have great success in the 1980s, especially since they composed songs which were to feature on TV soundtracks. *Harry's Game* brought them to the attention of a wider audience and it was the first Gaelic lyric to ever chart in Britain. They won a BAFTA for it. In 1984 they were commissioned to write the hauntingly atmospheric music for the television series *Robin of Sherwood* which also introduced Clannad to America and earned them another BAFTA award.

In 1993 Clannad embarked upon their first US tour which won standing ovations across the country. In 1996 they undertook an international tour, playing as far afield as Japan. During that same year they also received the Lifetime Achievement Award from the Irish Music Industry.

Maire Brennan is now an established solo artist, and emphasises heavily her love of Christianity. She has recently published a book called *The Other Side of the Rainbow*. The band continue to record and their music continues to gain new audiences.

One of the newest bands to emerge out of Ireland who play in both traditional and popular style are another family band called the Corrs.

The Corrs

The band grew up in the sort of town in Ireland where everyone knows everyone else. They were surrounded by music; their parents played in a local band and once their father Gerry realised the potential his offspring had they started taking piano lessons.

The Corrs consist of three sisters, Sharon (violin/vocals), Caroline (drums/bodhran/keyboards/vocals) and Andrea (lead vocals/tin whistle) and their brother Jim (guitar/keyboards/vocals). Jim as the eldest was the first to catch on to the piano and it was not long before he started playing guitar. Jim and Sharon began gigging locally alongside their parents in local pubs and bars around Dundalk in County Louth. They all got a break in the 1991 Alan Parker film *The Commitments* which is about the adventures of an Irish band. They all had parts in the movie, with Andrea playing the role of the lead character's sister. They were discovered by John Hughes during the filming and he went on to become their manager and put them under an apprenticeship to hone their repertoire and their stage act.

In 1994 the US ambassador to Ireland saw them playing at a small gig at Whelen's Music Bar in Dublin and invited them to Boston to play before the World Cup celebrations that year. In 1995 they released their debut album *Forgiven, Not Forgotten* which skilfully combined traditional Irish music with pop. The instrumental "Erin Shore" opened the album and before long the album hit over two million in sales, along with a non-stop tour to accompany it.

In 1996 Andrea appeared in another Alan Parker film, *Evita*, as Juan Peron's mistress. Their second album was also released although it was more pop-oriented than the first. They collaborated with outside songwriters and the Chieftains also recorded a cover of Jimi

Hendrix's "Little Wing" for the album's final track. Initial album sales were limited but after the Corrs had covered the Fleetwood Mac song "Dreams" which charted in the Top 10 the album rose to No 1 status in 1998.

Whilst most of the Corrs' single releases are pop music, their live performances and their albums still reflect their traditional Irish influence strongly. They have released a number of live videos too and Andrea Corr continues to do film work.

117

Above: The Corrs.

Above: The Corrs, brother and sisters band. 118

119

Story: Tom O'Sullivan

The story goes that in the early 1840s there was a German traveller touring Ireland. Nothing astounded him so much as the universal belief in the fairies and their potent influence on the affairs of mortals. One evening, after a céilí, held at the public house in a little village in County Sligo, he loudly stated his views.

"So your honour doesn't believe in our fairy stories?" asked one of the company. "Yet I'll lay a wager that there's a man now abroad to whom the strangest things have happened and which we must believe as they are plain, simple and indisputable facts. Now there's Tom O'Sullivan, your honour, there he stands and Tom, as you have heard, is one of the best bagpipe players in Kerry and Tom had never handled a bag of pipes in his life before he was 30. It happened one day, however, that good Tom was wandering among the hills and lay down to sleep in a place that belonged to the Good People, who we call the Sidhe. There are many such places in our country, as your honour has been told. Now as Tom lay sleeping, the fairies appeared to him and played him a selection of the most beautiful tunes upon their bagpipes and then they laid the bagpipes down by the side of him. Well, when Tom awoke, he found the bagpipes lying in the grass next to him and when he took them up he was able to play, offhand and quite pat, every one of the tunes that the fairies had taught him. Now that's a fact, your honour."

"Is it so, Tom?" enquired the traveller.

"Indeed it is, your honour," Tom answered. "And very pretty people they were that taught me and although it's now 30 years since they gave me the pipes, I have them still and they play as beautifully now as they did on the first day that I had them."

"There now, that's a fact your honour," interposed another of the company.

By way of strengthening the evidence to convince the incredulous German traveller, and after another round of whiskey punch that their skeptic had bought them, Tom went on and told him of a yet more marvellous adventure of a friend of his, one Phil McShane. McShane had fought in the great battle on the side of the Kerry fairies against the Limerick fairies and to reward his bravery the victors gave him a cap which, when worn, endowed him with the strength of seven men. "Phil has the cap still," continued Tom, "and when he puts it on there is not a man in the Barony who will affront him. Now that's another fact your honour and when you come to Kerry I will show you my pipes and my friend Phil will show you his cap."

"I see, sir, you don't believe in 'em," interrupted a young woman, "and yet it's a wonder ye don't. Well, I've seen them with my own eyes, dancing on the fairy grounds,

120

and I've heard their music too with my own ears, and beautiful music it is too."

After another round of whiskey punch, she continued with her tale. "Not long ago, while coming across the bog of Ballinasloe with my husband, both of us well tired, we laid down to rest by the side of the holy well there. My husband soon fell asleep but I did not and soon I heard the most delightful music. I thought surely there must have been a piper close at hand and stood up to look about me but I saw nothing. I waked my husband and bade him listen. He

says for us to go on and that it was just the good people playing and so, your honour ought to know at this time that there are fairies in Ireland and plenty of them and they have pipers and dancers just like us Christians, only better, and it isn't lucky for anyone, gentle or simple, to be laughing at them either."

And another round of whiskey punch followed, with more stories and more music and then another round of whiskey punch ... and the stories and the music continue.

Four Green Fields

"What did I have?" said the fine old woman
"What did I have?" this proud old woman did say
"I had four green fields, each one was a jewel
But strangers came and tried to take them from me
I had fine strong songs, they fought to save my jewels
They fought and died, and that was my grief" said she.

"Long time ago" said the fine old woman
"Long time ago" this proud old woman did say
"There was war and death, plundering and pillage
My children starved by mountain, valley and sea
and their wailing cries, they shook the very heavens
My four green fields ran red with their blood" said she.

"What have I now?" said the fine old woman
"What have I now?" this proud old woman did say
"I have four green fields, one of them's in bondage
In stranger's hands, that tried to take it from me
But my sons have sons, as brave as were their fathers
My fourth green field will bloom once again" said she.

Index

Index

Index

Index